W9-CJT-117

Strategies for Retiring Right!

MAY 2 0 2016

646.79 Atk

Atkinson, R.
Strategies for retiring right!

PRICE: $19.95 (3559/he   )

Strategies for Retiring Right!

Rick Atkinson

INSOMNIAC PRESS

Copyright © 2016 by Richard Atkinson

All rights reserved. No part of this publication may be reproduced, stored
in a retrieval system or transmitted, in any form or by any means, without
the prior written permission of the publisher or, in case of photocopying
or other reprographic copying, a license from
Access Copyright, 1 Yonge Street, Suite 1900,
Toronto, Ontario, Canada, M5E 1E5.

Cover design by Mike O'Connor. Cover image by iStockphoto.com.

Library and Archives Canada Cataloguing in Publication

Atkinson, Richard, 1941-, author
Strategies for retiring right! / Rick Atkinson.

Issued in print and electronic formats.
ISBN 978-1-55483-171-5 (paperback).--
ISBN 978-1-55483-185-2 (html)

1. Retirement. 2. Retirement--Planning. 3. Retirement--
Economic aspects. 4. Retirement--Psychological aspects. I. Title.

HQ1062.A85 2016   646.7'9   C2016-902027-4
                                         C2016-902028-2

Printed and bound in Canada

Insomniac Press, 520 Princess Ave.
London, Ontario, Canada, N6B 2B8
www.insomniacpress.com

Disclaimer

A. Financial Advice

The information included in this book is general in nature and is for educational purposes only. It does not constitute professional financial advice. Every effort has been made to ensure that the information provided is accurate, but individuals must not rely on this information to make any financial or investment decisions. Before making any such decision, it is recommended that you consult a qualified financial professional to take into account your particular investment objectives, financial situation, and individual needs.

B. Medical / Health Advice

The information included in this book is for educational purposes only. It is neither intended nor implied to be a substitute for professional medical advice. You should always consult your healthcare provider to determine the appropriateness of the information for your own situation or if you have any questions regarding a medical condition or treatment plan.

I dedicate this book to the many pre- and post-retirees who shared their insights and experiences with me. Your observations and stories both enriched my life and provided me with lessons to pass on to others.

Contents

Preface

There is life after work. You just have to find it and make certain you do it right! This is extremely important because retirement will likely be the second longest period of your life. And to help you make certain you're on the right path, I have written *Strategies for Retiring Right!*

While on the speaking circuit talking about my first book, *Don't Just Retire – Live It, Love It!* I was asked numerous times, "Rick, if you had to condense your retirement advice to six or seven major points, what would those be?" With this question reverberating in my mind, I sought the answer, which included speaking with the many successful retirees that I interviewed for my first book. As a result, *Strategies for Retiring Right!* was born. It's a practical guide offering profound insights, true stories, and hands-on exercises.

In its twenty-seven chapters, *Strategies for Retiring Right!* covers essential topics such as creating a holistic approach to retirement, understanding the need for a balanced leisure lifestyle, choosing where to live, taking charge of your retirement development, and following the seven strategies for retirement success, including using your concept of legacy to guide your actions in life after work.

Strategies for Retiring Right! is for anyone contemplating retirement, and the earlier you read it, the sooner you will be on the right path towards successful retirement planning. Even if you're already retired, the guidance this book offers will enhance the life you're leading and help you make certain you're getting the most out of your golden years.

Richard (Rick) Atkinson

Acknowledgements

I want to express my gratitude to the many people who helped make this book a reality. My appreciation extends back to the thousands who attended my presentations and workshops over the years. Their participation and feedback enabled me to hone my approach to this subject.

The personal stories that appear in this book have been gathered over many years from a variety of sources, some of whom I can't remember because they have become part of my lifetime concern with retirement. Other stories came from retirees and retirees-to-be.

The questions listed in Appendix B: Finding and Using a Financial Advisor were adapted from Gail Bebee's book *No Hype: The Straight Goods on Investing Your Money* (Ganneth, 2008).

A special shout-out to friends and acquaintances, including fellow members of the Tam Heather Venerables curling club (Canada's largest seniors curling club); members of Probus Canada, a social organization for those who are semi-retired or retired; and chapter members of CARP (formerly Canadian Association of Retired Persons), a national non-profit organization that advocates on behalf of adults over age fifty.

I would also like to thank Insomniac Press, in particular Mike O'Connor, who recognized the need for a book on the lifestyle side of retirement planning. Also thanks to Dan Varrette for his input and feedback on the manuscript. His organizational and planning skills added greatly to the success of the project.

A special thanks to my wife, Christine Edwards. She encouraged and supported this project from the very beginning.

Introduction

So you're thinking about retirement! Sitting at your desk or standing by your machine, you picture waking up in the morning when you're ready instead of when you have to; you lounge around the house with a cup of coffee and your favourite book; you call up friends for tennis or a round of golf, or maybe to play cards in the evening. Ah, freedom at last! You're no longer working. You're no longer commuting. For the first time in a long time, you're really enjoying life. Finally, you are retired!

When most people think about retirement, they imagine leaving a job they dislike, dropping out of the rat race and turning their back on the pressures of employment. They often see retirement as a welcome change or an escape to something more peaceful and serene. However, retiring is not only about giving up your job and spending your days relaxing; it's also about entering one of the most exciting and challenging stages of life. Retirement can be a time to draw upon your personal and professional experiences to open new doors of opportunity and education. It can be a time to realize your potential and accomplish significant goals that you delayed because of the responsibilities of working and raising a family.

The opportunities in retirement are endless; however, a successful retirement doesn't come without its hurdles. There are many considerations, such as living on a reduced income, creating a health and wellness strategy, examining and maintaining relationships with family and friends, allocating personal time, establishing living arrangements, adopting and adapting to different social roles, and adjusting to the eventual death of a partner, friends, and family members.

In your quest for a successful retirement, beware of retirement's outmoded image generating challenges of its own. Retirement used to mean starting a chapter in life in which retirees become non-productive, non-contributing members of society, heading into their final sunset. Many retirees still have this pessimistic view and end up mentally "hanging up their skates." They don't expect much from retirement, and, unfortunately, that's just what they get.

A Retirement Revolution

The good news is a quiet revolution has been taking place. Today's successful retirees are energized and are actively pursuing new life goals. By adopting a zest for life, no matter their circumstances, they are enthusiastic about the future and they shape their destiny as much as possible.

It's worth noting that the concept of living comfortably after retirement is a fairly new one. U.S. Social Security is only about eighty years old, and the Canada Pension Plan (CPP) is a little over fifty years young. Before the introduction of these systems, retirement was a luxury of the wealthy. Other people—most people—kept working until they couldn't any longer and often suffered after that point.

After World War II, as the middle class grew, so did the notion of retiring—of living comfortably after one stopped working. This in turn generated the concept of retirement planning.

In the beginning, the general focus of retirement planning was centred on money questions such as "How much will I need to retire comfortably?" "Will the money I've saved last long enough?" and "How much will I be able to pass on to my heirs?" As time went on, many realized that retirement is about much more than money and that planning for our non-monetary needs is also important. We need to plan what we'll do with our time. We also need to consider things such as maintaining or improving our health, and how we'll develop new social circles outside of work.

The importance of these things and more—a holistic approach—has become as vital as the financial issues for one simple reason: We're living longer!

Life Expectancy in Canada
Male age 65:   50% chance of living to 84
                    25% chance of living to 89

Female age 65:   50% chance of living to 88
                    25% chance of living to 92

Couple age 65:   50% chance one will live to 90
                    25% chance one will live to 94

Source: Canada at a Glance 2015, Statistics Canada

A Central Question and Personal Story
Most of us retiring today will live another fifteen, twenty, thirty, or more years. Retirement could be the second-longest period of our life. Considering this fact, I have a question for you:

Will you create the best retirement you can,
or will you let your retirement years just happen to you?

Letting retirement just happen is exactly what many people do, to the detriment of themselves and their loved ones. Let me share a personal story that illustrates the dangers of retiring without a well-thought-out plan.

My father, Jack, was more than merely successful in his work. He *loved* his job! His friends were there. His self-image was part of the job. His life happily revolved around work until the day he retired.

My father didn't have any hobbies or interests outside of his work. Like many others, his mental, physical, and emotional well-being was set adrift when he no longer had a job to go to. Eighteen months later, he passed away.

Naturally, this left a big impression on me. I was only twenty-four at the time and just starting my human resources career. Over the years, as a human resources professional, I observed hundreds of people move from active work to retirement. I eventually came to realize that the difference between thriving and failing to thrive in retirement was not about the money.

Unsuccessful Retirees

Unsuccessful retirees mainly see retirement as an escape. They picture retirement as the time they got rid of a job and/or boss they couldn't stand, finally having left behind the stress of long commutes and undesirable working conditions.

Unsuccessful retirees also tend to see retirement essentially as a vacation, and they try to fill their days the same way they did when on vacation. Unfortunately, vacation activities become boring—as well as expensive.

After a while, the vacation model fails and retirement no longer feels like an extended holiday. These retirees are then left with little to do that interests or engages them, and time begins to weigh heavily on their shoulders. Many of these retirees experience increased frustration and disappointment with their lives, caught up in a vortex they cannot or will not escape.

The problems these retirees experience are not generated by laziness or apathy. Rather, we can see the root causes in contrast to the factors that make successful retirees.

Successful Retirees
Successful retirees are often glad to leave their job, and they also look forward to having more time for the things they enjoyed when on vacation. However, successful retirees go far beyond that. They have a clear concept of what makes for a well-rounded, holistic, happy, and stimulating retirement. Many acquire that information from people who are already living a successful retirement. What's more, successful retirees apply that information in two key ways:

1. They build their own realistic and well-rounded vision of retirement.
2. They create and implement a plan to make it happen!

This book is designed to assist you to do the same. It outlines the issues you need to address, and it covers the best practices. My intent is to provide you with insight and direction without compromising your own decision-making process.

Part I of this book provides a model of a successful retirement. Its pages contain the knowledge, thoughts, and insights I've gleaned from interviews with hundreds of successful retirees. These are your virtual retirement mentors.

Part II helps you create your own unique retirement vision and plan. Although it can't do the work for you, Part II does provide support in implementing your plan to fulfill your vision.

So now the choice is yours. You can sit and wait for whatever comes along, or you can tackle the challenges and opportunities of retiring successfully. Will you reserve your place in the rocking chair or grab the brass ring of retirement life?

If you are somewhere between the ages of forty-five and sixty-five, it's time to explore your future as a retiree. Consider the contents of this book and take time to complete the exercises. Be sure to share your thoughts with your partner as you progress toward developing your personal retirement vision and plan.

Congratulations on being among those who take a proactive interest in your retirement. I wish you all the best in developing a plan that enriches your life.

Kindest regards,
Richard (Rick) Atkinson

Part I
Strategies for Retiring Right

Chapter 1

What Is Your Current Picture?

So where do you start in planning for retirement? I suggest you start by taking time to consider and visualize what retirement *currently* means to you. Do whatever you usually do when you want to think things over, whether it's sitting quietly by yourself, taking a walk, or chatting with a friend over coffee.

Don't attempt to complete this exercise in one sitting. Give yourself several opportunities to bring your current images of retirement to mind. In my interviews with successful retirees, every one of them said that thinking through what retirement means can take several days or weeks.

Your images and thoughts probably won't be well-rounded, coherent, or complete—that's not the point of visualizing your retirement. Rather, the point is to reveal the strengths you already have so you can build on them as well as reveal the negatives so you can deal with them.

Do you need some help or inspiration to get your thought process rolling?

Write It Down

Although there's no need to organize your thoughts at this time, you might want to write down your current picture of the things you look forward to, have concerns about, etc. In fact, I recommend it. This not only gives you something to use as you move ahead; it also emulates one of the key strategies successful retirees use: writing things down.

Food for Thought
What is it about retirement that attracts, scares, or excites you? The answer to this question—the positive and negative thoughts or images of retirement—are as individual as you are. However, here are some specific questions to help you get started:

- Are you looking forward to getting up when you want instead of when the alarm rings?
- Do you want to spend more time with your grandchildren, your partner, or other family members? Are you concerned about being expected to do that?
- Does retirement mean you're getting "old"?
- Does retirement mean leaving work you love?
- Is there a significant difference between retiring on your own timeline versus being forced or asked to take early retirement?
- Are you looking forward to having more time to take care of yourself?
- What does retirement mean when it comes to doing things you've wanted to do for years?
- Do you find it hard to imagine what you'll do with your time?
- Does your partner express concern or joke about you "being in their way" (or vice versa)?

In general, couples should complete this exercise

separately. It's quite common to have more negative images and thoughts than positive ones, so don't worry if this is the case for you. Understanding the situation makes it easier to change things for the better down the road. I recommend you write down your thoughts—whether positive or negative, whether cohesive or not—and keep them for future reference.

Chapter 2

Overview — The Holistic Approach

In many ways, we can consider current and soon-to-be retirees only the second generation to experience retirement. And, as noted in the Introduction, the nature of retirement is undergoing a transformation. Although the change is positive, it still means that many of us aren't sure just what elements we need in place and lack role models we can easily emulate. The following chapters cover these elements, the pieces that together—holistically—make a successful retirement. In overview, you will need:

- A definition or image of your new role: How you see yourself in retirement
- A balanced leisure lifestyle: How you spend your time
- A place to live: Where you spend your time

Successful retirees also teach us that the above must be realistic. For example, your ideal retirement might include living in a new home closer to your grandchildren so you can spend more time with them. However, should the state of the housing market prevent such a move at the time, your vision and plan need to include your current home or some other alternative. That doesn't mean you should put your hopes of moving aside forever—quite the opposite! Few aspects of your plan and retired life will or should be static over time.

Successful retirees also tell me they take steps to nurture the following:

- A positive attitude
- Good mental and physical health
- Spirituality

Note the word *nurture*; many people acknowledge they had to work a bit harder at some of the above once they retired. Successful retirees make the effort rather than wait for outside influences to do the work for them.

A successful retirement also includes applying certain strategies along the way. These strategies are:

- *Apply the idea of your desired legacy.* Imagining what you want to be remembered for can help guide today's choices.
- *Enhance relationships and communication.* Major life changes almost always affect relationships, and retirement is no exception.
- *Find and use mentors.* Success rarely occurs in a vacuum!
- *Document the plan, process, and progress.* Writing things down is a best practice among all successful retirees.
- *Share successes.* This book is informed by stories, comments, and ideas that many successful retirees and those on the path to success have shared. You'll see some of these within each chapter, and we'll begin with comments about an issue that runs as a thread throughout a successful retirement: your new role.

Your New Role

For many of us in North America, work is a defining feature of our life, and this begins at a very young age. Children play with work roles such as teacher or soldier. They dress up in work attire for Halloween: doctors, astronauts—even pirates are pirates for a living.

Work is also closely linked to our very identity and self-image. Adults ask children what they want to "be" when they grow up, and the accepted answer is generally linked to a particular type of work. The focus on work-as-identity continues through adulthood. When we ask, "What do you do?" we mean to ask what one does for a living. Upon retirement, however, this focus has quite different implications for our self-image.

Our preoccupation with work helps generate the image of retirement as comprising little more than sitting in a rocking chair and watching the world pass us by. Even today, many think being a retiree means being a non-productive, non-contributing member of society. This pitfall often takes people by surprise.

I am a nurse about four months from retirement. As I listened to your presentation, I realized I felt extremely depressed because I, too, equated retirement with the end of "usefulness." Luckily, the message that retirement didn't have to be that way has sunk in. I am ready to create my own "useful" next phase. I know this sounds like an exaggeration, but it's entirely sincere. You saved my life!
—Wilma F.

It's also common for people who enjoyed their work to think they'll retain the satisfaction of past years, resting on their laurels, so to speak. This, too, is a mistake.

A young man (Charlie) and I chatted while waiting to board a plane. He asked what I do; I responded by talking about my work. About halfway into my explanation, he seemed to realize I was talking about work I did years ago. The look on his face changed from one of interest to one of dismissal. Suddenly, I felt oddly irrelevant, and the feeling bothered me for several days.
— Rick A., author

Of course, many people retire from work they did not enjoy; however, their former role can still create problems.

My husband did not enjoy his work, but when he retired, he seemed to apply his former role of manager to me. This created a number of arguments that ended with me begging him to find something to get him out of the house. It wasn't until he angrily pointed out I kept referring to the house as "my" house that I realized I, too, needed to make some adjustments.
—Rita A., homemaker

Don't let these pitfalls trip you up. A successful retirement includes focusing on what you now "do," not just on what you used to do. Thinking of yourself as a retired su-

pervisor, manager, professor, or nurse—or just plain retired—is limiting.

What's Next?

When you retire, it's time to write a new "job description."
It's time to develop and strengthen your ability to find satisfaction in new interests and pursuits. That's not to say
you should ignore what you used to do for a living, but
it's time to include grandparent, gardener, artist, photographer, speed walker, student, avid reader, budding nov-
elist, etc., to your description.

You might not have a new role already in mind when
you retire. That's okay because many people don't. However, if you simply wait for something interesting to show
up, you'll find yourself on a slippery slope to an unhappy,
unsuccessful retirement. You've got time to explore and
try new things, to develop your new role(s) or sense of
self. The key is to be proactive, which you can do as you
build a balanced leisure lifestyle.

Chapter 3

The Need for a
Balanced Leisure Lifestyle

Gone are the days of rushing to work, fighting traffic, meeting deadlines, skipping lunch, and working overtime. Retirement is the time to slow down, relax, and play. This is your reward for all your years of hard work. The question for you now is this: What are you going to *do* with your leisure time?

It's quite common for new retirees to spend many months in at-home vacation mode. It feels great to not have to set an alarm. It's nice to pull on jeans instead of a suit. It's wonderful to hit the links when the course isn't busy, to read the books that have been piling up on the nightstand. These retirees think they can pull off total unstructured leisure. But can you imagine playing golf six or seven times a week, or watching TV for hours at a time? Most of us would begin to hate the game, or would eventually want to throw the TV out the window.

After years of enjoying golf only once a month (if I was lucky), I looked forward to playing as often as I wanted. Joined the local club. Entered every tournament. Bugged my working buddies to play hooky and went on as a single when that didn't work. I was thrilled to see my game improve, but after a couple months, my scores crept up. Lessons

didn't help. Eventually, I realized that I was bored.
—Reg H., former manager

In addition to attempting to live in vacation mode, it's very common for new retirees to tackle their "honey-do list" with unprecedented gusto: clear out the garage and sewing room; fix the squeaky doors; paint the spare bedroom; hang the new curtains; weed, plant, repot. But even if you have a very long list, you'll eventually run out of things that need doing around the house.

> *When I retired, I immediately began to address a long list of repairs and improvements in my home. Immediately! This was quite gratifying, at first. But when my daughter laughingly accused me of repeating to-dos, I had to acknowledge she was right. I did not know what to do with my time.*
> —Cecil D., former tool and die maker

The Hazards of Leisure Time

When we run out of things to do, we often begin to lose our sense of self, our feeling of usefulness. We often also lose structure in terms of time, and largely unstructured days, for days on end, can have negative effects. This is true at any age, as those of you who raised children can attest. For adults, especially older adults, the negative effects can include anxiety and even depression.

These negative effects tend to accumulate slowly over time and can be extremely difficult to recognize. This is just one reason why proactively building a balanced leisure lifestyle is so important. So just what does *balanced* mean?

Building Balance

A balanced leisure lifestyle includes at least one regular activity in each of these categories:

1. Entertainment
2. Education
3. Travel
4. Exercise
5. Social activities
6. Hobbies

Let's take a look at how you can build balance.

1. Entertainment

Entertainment stimulates your mind and provides healthy diversions and amusement—laughter is good for the soul. There are many activities that fall into the entertainment category. The activity should be something meaningful, but this doesn't mean it has to be expensive. Suitable entertainment includes:

- Attending concerts, films, plays, and sporting events
- Watching your favourite films and TV shows at home
- Dining out
- Attending fairs, festivals, or other special events
- Hosting dinner parties or get-togethers to play cards or other tabletop games
- Going on a regular date night (or day) to have a special dinner and/or do something special together

We're very lucky to live in an area with lots of entertainment, including plenty of low-cost or free

entertainment. We go to street fairs, see community theatre, attend "afternoons at the opera." Turns out we quite like opera!
—Susan M., former accountant

My girlfriends and I used to struggle to find time to get together. Now that we're all retired, we've made a point to do something fun together once a month. We rotate who chooses the event or activity, which has generated some interesting variety.
—Bev. S., former teacher

Note: Many people enjoy reading one or two books a week or watching certain TV shows. However, spending too much time doing things like this can make these activities more of a way to pass the time. These activities should be special entertainment.

2. Education
You need to continue to give yourself opportunities to learn. This not only gives your brain stimulation; it also energizes your sense of adventure and discovery. Common educational activities include:

- Learn a new language
- Learn a new craft
- Research your genealogy
- Become a tour guide at a local museum
- Attend lectures, workshops, and seminars
- Take cooking classes
- Read challenging non-fiction

Most communities in North America offer many resources for educational activities. These opportunities become even vaster when you include online options. If you live near a community college or university, see what programs they offer. Check with your local community recreation department, and senior centres too. Try to have at least one educational activity in your lifestyle mix at all times.

I asked my nephew to show me how to use my computer and go on the Internet. We started out slowly, and I could barely use the mouse. One evening, he showed me a "blog," and I jokingly said that considering how opinionated I am, I should have one. Well, now he's teaching me how to do that!
—Peter T., former small business owner

My family emigrated from Ecuador to Canada when I was just a baby. My parents were fluent in both Spanish and English but purposely used English to help my siblings and me assimilate quickly. (They also used Spanish when they hoped to keep their conversation private, which of course did not work perfectly.) Your comments about education have reawakened an interest in improving my Spanish.
—Arturo W., architect

3. Travel
Most successful retirees I've interviewed mention the importance of including travel as part of a balanced leisure

lifestyle. When we travel, we acquire different perspectives of the world, whether it's travelling to the next province or state, a nearby country, or around the globe. Learning more about our world, and its people and events, enriches our lives.

Travelling also helps us develop mental and emotional flexibility because we usually encounter the unexpected along the way. This, in turn, helps us handle the unexpected at home with less stress.

Travel opportunities are numerous, especially since retirees have more time. And, as with entertainment, travel need not be expensive. Although some people love to take a cruise a couple of times a year, or participate in group tours to exotic destinations, there are many inexpensive ways to travel, including:

- Participating in bus tours of nearby places
- Driving a few miles to stay with old friends
- Taking an annual camping trip

Many successful retirees with modest incomes recommend saving up to take "big" trips every few years or so (as in the example below). So go see your sister in Manitoba. Take that cruise to Alaska. Go camping. See Italy. Visit the kids.

My wife and I decided to act as if we were tourists in our own city. We made a list of all the places we'd take guests but didn't necessarily go to on our own. It's been great fun to see the sights again and rediscover the entire region. We also take day

and overnight trips to new places described in a "tourists" guide.
—Wilson G., former machinist

I have always wanted to go to Italy. When my granddaughter entered high school, I started saving for a trip for the both of us that we'd take if she graduated with honours. She and I have been planning for four years. I'm delighted to say our plans and her grades are on track for a wonderful trip.
—Lily V., former bus driver

4. Exercise

Every retiree needs regular exercise. You should include at least one exercise component in your leisure plan. Whether you choose to hike, bike, golf, swim, fish, play tennis, do yoga, or power walk, you will benefit from some activity that helps you stay physically fit.

Don't let physical or financial limitations hold you back. There are many options for inexpensive exercise you can do at home, including types for people with limited mobility. Tai chi, yoga, and chair- and water-based exercise are just a few.

Though I was fairly fit until my late forties, I developed asthma and lost the desire to push myself. Once the newness of retirement had eased, I forced myself to take regular slow walks around the local park. I made friends with others doing the same, which helped me follow through and develop a good habit. The walking also had a surprising effect in that my asthma became less of a problem than it had been in years!

—Bo W., former restaurant owner

Not wanting to squeeze myself into an embarrassing Lycra outfit, I checked out several exercise videos from the library. I tried yoga, light weights, and tai chi in the comfort of my own home. I got hooked on one of those silly Sweatin' to the Oldies *programs, which I found in a thrift store. I'm dancing (and sweating) twice a week.*

—Phillis A., former decorator

Be sure to consult with your doctor before beginning any new exercise. You might also want to ask for activity suggestions. Many health centres offer exercise classes, light equipment (e.g., resistance bands), and discounts for gyms.

When choosing your exercise, consider choosing one for the warmer months and another one for the colder months. That way, inclement weather will not become an excuse to stop.

If you haven't been physically active in a while (or at all), make the effort to find an activity you actually enjoy. Otherwise, your commitment will most likely dwindle.

As you look for the right kind of exercise, be sure to try a variety of different activities before committing to one. During the testing period, refrain from buying expensive equipment in case the activity you initially enjoyed turns out not to be something you want to continue. The same suggestion applies to exercise videos: rent or borrow (from family, friends, or the library) before you buy, if possible.

Finally, beware of high-pressure sales tactics at gyms. Look for gyms that allow you to do a brief trial period or join on a month-to-month basis.

5. Social Activities

Interacting with others is important at all stages of life. As social beings, we fulfill our social needs by participating in activities that involve other people. When we retire, we leave many associations behind, and we also lose convenient places to build friendships, share common interests, and enjoy the company of others. Most people don't realize the extent to which co-workers help fill the basic need for socialization—the lunchtime talks, coffee breaks, company and industry events, grabbing a drink after work—and often find themselves feeling lonely without knowing why.

It's important to replace, as best as possible, the shared time you had through work with other social activities that provide fellowship. This is important even if your work relationships were not particularly satisfying. Either way, you now have the opportunity to vastly improve on your situation.

Joining a service or social club can be a great way to fill this need. Such groups usually bring in new members in ways that make it easier for even shy people to begin developing new relationships. Consider groups such as Lions Clubs International, Optimist International, or Rotary International. You might want to consider Probus

Clubs, an offshoot of Rotary intended for retired and semi-retired people.

Also consider joining or continuing your membership in a professional association linked to your past work. Most groups welcome retired members, especially because retirees have more time to fill those vital volunteer roles.

Other ways to develop a social circle and participate in activities include volunteering in the planning and implementation of events such as annual parades, charity walks, and so on. You might even want to join the board of directors connected with these events.

There are plenty of non-business social groups too, including book clubs, ham radio clubs, knitting circles, hiking clubs, motorcycle clubs, etc.

Last but certainly not least, regular attendance in an exercise class means socializing with others who do the same.

Being active in such groups will fulfill your social activity needs, but it often meets your education and exercise needs too. The important thing is to get out there and participate, socialize, meet new people, and make new friends. If you're not used to being very social, you might need to push yourself. Don't let isolation creep up on you.

Every morning, I went down to the corner coffee shop for coffee and a sweet. Some sort of club (Optimist International, as I later learned) was there every other Wednesday. Though I had not been much of a "joiner" in the past, I found myself more than half-listening to the speakers and nodding hello to the regular attendees. It seemed natural to inquire about membership and then finally to join. It's a great pleasure to develop friendships with these fine people. I also enjoy participating in activities designed to give back to our local community.

—Dan S., former financial advisor

Our church has an unusual Bible study group. Since we read and discuss books on many religions, it's closer to a comparative religion course with a good deal of political discussion thrown in. The group is open to anyone over the age of eighteen, which makes for an interesting mix in the discussion.

—Mitchell O., former carpenter

6. Hobbies

Successful retirees emphasize the importance of having at least one hobby. One of the greatest benefits is the pleasure of working at something without having any obligation to do so. Many people enjoy hobbies that produce something in particular. It can be very satisfying to learn and refine one's ability to make something, even if that something exists for only a short time—as with cooking meals or arranging flowers. Engaging in craftsmanship and artistry can be greatly rewarding.

Meeting the mental and physical challenges associated with many hobbies can be quite satisfying as well. For example, it takes mental skill to calculate the amount of fabric needed for a quilt or to adjust a woodworking pattern.

Bird watchers must analyze the flora to find the birds they seek, as well as trek far and wide.

Hobbies are yet another thing for which there are many options. Here are some others in addition to those already mentioned:

- Painting or drawing
- Knitting or other needlecrafts
- Restoring cars, furniture, etc.
- Making wine or beer.
- Running a doll "hospital"
- Photography
- Gardening
- Model building
- Scrapbooking
- Beading or jewelry-making

As with choosing an exercise activity, be sure to make the effort to see if you do indeed enjoy a particular hobby before making any expensive purchases. In addition, don't expect a hobby to interest you forever. If your interest wanes, try to find a new hobby.

My wife's car has a bumper sticker on it: "You can't have too much fabric." She's a quilting maniac. Used to drive me crazy. Then I got into woodworking, and now I get it.
—Johnathan Z., former banker

My husband used to tease me about the amount of fabric in our spare room—my sewing room. I convinced him to apply his new hobby of woodworking to make some quilt hangers and stands. They are beautiful! We've been selling my quilts and his stands at local flea markets, farmers' markets, and

*craft fairs. Doesn't make us a mint, of course, but
it's enough to feed our hobbies and keep him quiet.*
—Marsha Z. fabric designer

Finding the right combination of entertainment, education, travel, exercise, social activities, and hobbies to match your lifestyle and personality takes time and effort. It might take some practice to develop the inward discipline to get yourself up early to join the local mall walkers. You might find that at first it takes extra effort to turn off the TV and go to the lunch meeting of a local volunteer group. Regardless, if you make the effort, you'll be glad you did.

Experiment and Adjust Over Time
Be prepared to experiment with your leisure activity selection until you find the right mix. Be prepared to make adjustments over time, too, as the opportunities and your interests change. You might also need to make adjustments as your physical or financial situations change. Don't let new challenges deter you!

*My knees became so bad I could barely walk up
and down stairs. Though I knew going to the pool
for water exercise would help, the thought of dealing with the ladder was too much, and I stopped
going. Two weeks later, a friend from class called
to see if I was okay. After hemming and hawing
over the reason for my absence, I finally confessed.
To my surprise, she laughed and laughed and then
reminded me she herself uses the lift to get in and*

out. I went back the next week and only suffered from being teased.
—Norma E., artist

Some of your activities might fall into more than one category. For example, taking classes associated with a hobby could meet an education need, and chatting with fellow hobby aficionados could meet social needs too.

However, don't let the category crossovers go too far, or your lifestyle might be balanced only on paper. Just because your set design hobby puts you inside a community theatre doesn't mean you've also met the need for entertainment.

Balance for Couples
Couples occasionally try to establish a leisure lifestyle in which they do everything together. Although this works for some couples, most find it impossible to achieve in a healthy way. There is good reason for that: Being a couple doesn't mean both people have identical interests and needs.

Just as everyone should experiment to find the right mix of activities, couples should experiment to find the right balance of things they do together and things they do separately. It's also important for couples to communicate about this. Discuss expectations, any feelings of exclusion, and budget issues.

Procrastination Stops You Before You Even Get Started
The greatest impediment to creating a balanced leisure life is procrastination. We sometimes tell ourselves, "I'll start

my search next month," but then this elusive "next month" never comes.

Some retirees find that such procrastination eventually becomes unhealthy. They describe becoming gradually disenchanted with retirement. Some even sink deeply into isolation and develop a habit of low expectations. To avoid these problems, I recommend using a calendar to set review points.

Place notes in your calendar three months, six months, nine months, and one year after your retirement date. Each note should read, "Am I living a balanced and satisfactory life? If not, create and implement my plan for a successful retirement now." These reminders should help you keep procrastination at bay, and they will even allow you to revise your plan based on your experiences, whether positive or negative, but remember: Planning is one thing, but it's taking action that counts.

Don't put off your search. Start checking out the fun stuff and get building your leisure plan today!

Chapter 4
Working and Volunteering

Many successful retirees work at paid and/or volunteer jobs. One of the benefits of working in retirement is a greater appreciation of your leisure hours. Retirees report that money jobs and volunteering also help eliminate their down periods, especially if they have too much leisure time on their hands. Another reported benefit is the therapeutic value of keeping mentally and physically sharp.

Through working and volunteering, you might also meet compatible people—people with similar interests and perspectives as yours. This can lead to developing new friendships and widening your social circle.

Working and volunteering might also provide you with opportunities to showcase your professional or trade skills as well as learn new ones. This can give you a great sense of accomplishment and can even lead to new careers.

Nobody ever asked Picasso when he was going to retire, and I'm not going to fully retire either. I'm just getting much pickier about the kinds of projects I take on.
—Jim N., consultant

My daughter recently commented—complained a bit—that I am never at home these days. She's right! Since becoming involved in the Showcase

[charity event], I am at meetings, reviewing ven-
ues, recruiting, and training other volunteers,
among other things. I have not worked this hard
for a while, but I am having a blast.
—Vince F., former human resources practitioner

Working at a Money Job

Many retirees continue to work for a paycheque either by choice or out of necessity. If either of these situations applies to you, you might want to begin with your former employer. Employers are becoming more amenable to employing senior employees, including on a contract basis. If that's not an option or your preference, seek out new types of work. Consider seasonal work such as working in retail shops during the holidays or working at a lakeside resort in the summer.

My best employees are retirees and former cus-
tomers. These guys and gals know their stuff and
the [hardware] store inside and out. They're reli-
able and provide the old-fashioned customer serv-
ice we want.
—Gora A., business owner

The number of options depends somewhat on where you live (and the economy). Do some research and be willing to step outside of your comfort zone. Here are some of the money jobs that might be available:

- Tutor
- Retail clerk

- Substitute teacher
- Courtesy shuttle driver for an automotive repair shop or a hotel
- Customer service representative
- Office assistant

Retirement savings and pensions make ends meet, but that's about all. I have worked at several part-time jobs over the past few years. My paycheques go toward having some fun as well as the unexpected little things.
—Mable K., former auto assembler

When looking for paid work, be extremely cautious with job offers that seem too good to be true, especially those that require you to contribute money upfront. Common examples of scams include "jobs" stuffing envelopes and assembling items from home.

Retirement might also be the time you've been waiting for to start your own business. The options are limitless and include consulting in your former field of work. Here are some other examples of careers retirees have started:

- Tax preparation
- Real estate agent
- Event planning
- Child care
- Cake decorating
- Home staging
- Computer repair
- Photographer
- Pet sitting
- Executive coaching
- Small engine repair
- Home inspection

Caution: Working for pay can affect your tax situation. Consult with a knowledgeable advisor *before* accepting or beginning paid work.

Volunteering

Many retirees will tell you the thing they miss the most from their working lives is the structure. They miss the need to be at work for a certain time, attending meetings, solving problems, being with people, and working toward goals. If you crave any of these things but don't wish to find a money job, then volunteering might be for you.

Volunteering has many other valuable benefits besides providing you with structure. As human beings, we have a strong need to help others. Volunteering makes us feel needed and useful, and it provides us with a sense of purpose. Helping others develop and succeed gratifies us.

When I visited my new great-grandson in the hospital, I noticed several people about my age holding and rocking infants in the nursery. When I learned that this simple act helps at-risk babies have a good chance at a healthy life, I volunteered. Does me good as well.
— Yvonne F., former businesswoman

Volunteering also gives us a tremendous sense of pride from earning the respect of others. We enjoy being appreciated and recognized for our efforts. Volunteering can also help us develop new skills and open doors to opportunities!

I love gardening and volunteered on the weekends at our local botanical centre. When I retired and was there more often, people began to ask if they could hire me to design their garden. I now offer

services in small garden design, especially using native plants.
—Gail B., former sr. nurse

The options for volunteering are limitless, but here are some examples:

- Teaching English or other languages, or teaching adults to read
- Assisting children with math and other school subjects
- Delivering meals to shut-ins
- Counselling young mothers, new business owners, or disadvantaged youth
- Participating in programs such as Habitat for Humanity
- Being a starter and/or marshal at a golf course (usually earns free rounds)

Manage Your Time

When considering volunteering, ask yourself, "How much time do I want to commit?" Is the answer three hours a day, one morning a week, or two days a week? Once you decide what makes sense for you, stick to your time allocation until you're sure you can and want to handle more.

You also need to learn to say no because volunteer organizations are constantly looking for additional help. It's easy to find yourself bombarded with requests, and you can easily become overwhelmed. If requests for your time and talent grow to be too much, don't be afraid to say, "Thanks but no thanks." Learn how to disengage yourself completely if the hours become too much or if the organization is not to your satisfaction.

Working or Volunteering Is Rarely Enough

The most significant hazard of working or volunteering is being lulled into thinking that it will be enough to generate a successful retirement. It won't.

Most retirees who work for a paycheque or volunteer still find their lives have significantly changed, especially because most work or volunteer only part-time. There is, however, still a great need to actively plan and manage your *leisure* time. In other words, planning and implementing a balanced retired life is still important. As the comment below illustrates, developing such a balance can be important whether one is retired or not.

> *My goal in bringing my father to your program was to encourage him to do something besides watch TV. I believe it will help him, but I have to say your comments hit home for me as well. I plan to use the list of "balance" to make some changes.*
> —Clint B., postal worker

Chapter 5
Choosing Where to Live

Considering where you will spend your time is every bit as important as considering how you will spend your time.

Many retirees hope their current home will meet their retirement needs, or, rather, it's more accurate to say many retirees prefer to stay in their current home. They like the neighbourhood and want to stay close to friends, children, and grandchildren. They are comfortable in the residence and like the climate. Staying in their current home also often gives them the advantage of being close to professionals and services they know already (e.g., doctors, hairstylists, etc.).

For many reasons, including familiarity, our home is often where we feel the most safe and secure. Unfortunately, hope, preference, and/or familiarity prompt some retirees to skip over a key step: giving serious thought to the financial repercussions of moving versus staying put. A bit of historical context will explain why retirees fail to take this important step.

A Change in How We Own Our Home
Before the cost of homeownership increased so substantially, most homeowners had a goal of paying off their home mortgage within a certain time frame. Many were able to reach this goal before or close to the time they retired, which made their housing expenses in retirement

comparatively low.

Owning a home free and clear is far less realistic these days. Making regular (and substantial) mortgage payments has become the norm, and many of today's retirees fail to consider the repercussions of carrying such an expense. What's more, despite the recent housing market meltdown, many homeowners see their home as an asset that can be used to cover expenses if the need arises. They fail to consider that tapping into this equity also means increasing debt.

Don't make these mistakes. Take the time to do the math, and be sure to get expert advice and guidance on these issues, including the pros and cons of reverse mortgages.

With a reverse mortgage, a homeowner takes out a loan based on the equity and market value of the home. Any current mortgage is paid off with the proceeds, and the bank makes either a lump sum or monthly payments to the homeowner with the remaining funds. Alternatively, the homeowner can set up a line of credit with the proceeds of the reverse mortgage to draw on when necessary. The homeowners retains the title to their home and remain responsible for paying real estate taxes and homeowner's insurance. The homeowner is required to have mortgage insurance for the reverse mortgage loan.

Financial Planning 101

Many people don't know how much they spend each month. Take the time to itemize monthly household expenses and other spending.

To qualify for a reverse mortgage, the homeowner must continue to live in the residence as their main home. The interest rate on the loan is variable, and the reverse mortgage doesn't have to be repaid as long as the homeowner stays in the home.

Satisfaction and Suitability Over Time

Think about your true level of satisfaction regarding your current home as well as its suitability as you age. Consider the following:

- Is your home an appropriate size for your planned retirement situation?
- Is your home easy to maintain on your own? If not, how much would reliable assistance cost?
- Does your home have a good layout? Will it easily accommodate walkers and/or wheelchairs?
- Do you like your neighbours and the neighbourhood?
- Do you have friends nearby? Do they plan to stay in the area?
- Do you live near siblings, children, grandchildren, or other family members who can be of assistance? Do you get along fairly well?
- Is the climate appealing? Does the area have satisfying greenery and/or other beautification? Is the area quiet enough for your standards?
- Is there easy access to common venues such as restaurants, cafés, retail shops, community centres, fitness centres, parks, and scenic walks?
- Is there easy access to everyday needs such as grocery stores and pharmacies?

- Is there easy access to medical and dental care?
- Does the area have adequate roads and sidewalks? Is it well-illuminated at night?
- Does the area have adequate public transportation or other options if you don't wish to or can no longer drive?

It's vital to consider the above issues ahead of time. Doing so not only prevents serious problems in the future; it can also improve your life here and now.

I've owned a cottage on the coast for many years. I was very much looking forward to moving there once retired. It's a lovely, quiet place, just the right size. I happen to have a heart condition. Your comments about living miles from medical facilities are well taken. I will discuss the issues with my doctor and research more thoroughly before deciding whether to retire there or not.
—Bibi F., government employee

Do I like where I now live, or am I simply used to it? Good question!
—Peter B., writer

Research Before Moving

Should you decide to move from your current home, take time to research your move first, whether you're considering a move across town, across the province or state, or to another country.

There are several ways to conduct this research, including taking an extended holiday or renting in the potential location. If you choose to only visit or spend an extended holiday, make sure you do so at different times of the year so you get an idea of the full experience.

If you are considering moving into a retirement community or "aging in place" residence, do your research by spending many hours there. Most places will even allow you to stay on a short-term or month-to-month basis.

Ensure a Strong Joint Decision

Remember, too, that this is a joint decision if you're living with someone! I've met countless people who have learned this the hard way, including a couple who almost divorced on their way to fulfilling the husband's dream.

The husband had always dreamed of touring North America. Once they both had retired, they sold their home, stuck their furniture and household goods in storage, bought a gorgeous fifth-wheel trailer and a truck to pull it, and took off. When I met them, they were indeed very close to divorcing! Living in the confined space of the trailer was driving them both crazy. In addition, the wife secretly felt she'd been talked into this unhappy adventure.

The lesson? They should have kept their house, rented a trailer, and experimented with living together in a small space as they roamed a few nearby counties. They should have also talked honestly with each other before hitting the road.

If you're in a relationship, you should both take time to reflect on your own hopes, dreams, and everyday preferences. Once you're both certain that you've adequately shared your wants and needs with each other, you should then discuss the issues honestly. Be open and willing to compromise. If you run into roadblocks, seek input from others to help identify solutions.

Helping Achieve Balance

Give yourself the opportunity to review all factors of your move before taking the leap. As you do your research, think about the aspects of your new home that will help with your balanced leisure lifestyle. In addition to the considerations listed above regarding your current home, consider the following:

- Is entertainment within easy reach both financially and logistically?
- Will it be easy to meet and make new friends, or will it be hard to break into the local social scene?
- Will it be easy for family and friends to visit you from afar?
- Will it be easy to obtain a new doctor and/or dentist?
- Is there convenient access to the educational pursuits and exercise activities that you are currently engaged in or hope to begin sometime during your retirement?
- Is the community suitable for enjoying your hobby or will you have to find a new one?

Moving and the Art of Downsizing

Reducing housing expenses often requires moving to a smaller home. Such downsizing might be a positive and practical choice for living a simpler life, but it still requires exploration and forethought.

When downsizing, don't try to take all your current

possessions and stuff them into your new, smaller home. Rightsize before you move! Examine your furniture and other goods with a critical eye. Make decisions about the big pieces first, but don't stop there. Glean through clothes, books, housewares, etc. Now is the time to unload other people's things too, including items you've stored for your children. Have the rightful owners come pick these items up. Having a garage sale and making donations to a charity will also help lighten the load.

Don't get stuck moving unneeded items into a smaller home, as it will make it feel cramped and confining before you even have a chance to make it feel comfortable. You also want to avoid paying for unnecessary storage space if possible.

Also consider hiring a professional organizer. Working with a professional organizer can reduce stress and help you reach your goals more quickly. However, many people can handle the process of downsizing themselves, especially if a friend or family member helps. Do-it-yourselfers should set a deadline well before any downsizing must be complete. That way, if things don't move forward as planned, you'll still have time to hire some help.

If you get stuck or overwhelmed by the process and run out of time, simply put the things you're not sure about in storage. Consider using storage areas that aren't easy to access in your new home. Having to work hard to get to things will help you determine if you really want or need them, making it easier to complete your downsizing.

Chapter 6

Developing Personal
Traits for Success

In talking with retirees, it's clear to me that attitude, mental health, and spirituality often make the difference between a successful and an unsuccessful retirement. The two stories below, one shared with me by a retiree's best friend, illustrate this.

I am officially bubbly, the one friends call for cheering up. Even my work [flight attendant] was generally upbeat. For some reason, I found it very hard to see the bright side when I retired. Molehills became mountains. I felt stuck in my little apartment because my budget was so tight. Then my sister persuaded me to fly out and visit her. Making the trip "required" me to smile and engage with people. That's when I realized I had simply gotten out of the practice of being happy.
—Linda H., retired flight attendant

I am Keith's best friend. In fact, I may now be his only friend. When Keith retired, he went from a tolerable Eeyore to extremely bitter. He only talks about his "lost" job and work buddies, all of whom have pretty much dumped him. His negative attitude about "getting old" and his many complaints about everything from kids in the neighbourhood to the cost of frozen dinners have driven a lot of people away. Keith spends many hours alone, mostly because he turns down all of my invitations to go do something. His kids visit only when they have to. I'm hanging in there for now, but don't know how much longer that will last.

—Shaun R., foundry worker

Those who have an innate positive attitude and strong spirituality still find retirement presents new challenges. Those who tend to be sullen face even greater challenges. This chapter is intended to prepare you for these challenges and help you overcome them. Take charge of your development.

The Power of Attitude

Fear, panic, and discomfort are common emotions experienced by people preparing for or entering retirement. These emotions often occur because retiring is like entering a new world—one with different circumstances, behaviours, and activities. It is a world filled with change: changing routines and activities, changing relationships, and changing responsibilities. Our attitude toward these changes makes a tremendous difference.

For some people, retirement is so overwhelming that they consciously or subconsciously sabotage their retirement plan by adopting a negative attitude. They feel "it's all over," that the changes required are too hard, and they visualize failure. Many look back at their life as the "good old days" rather than welcoming the adventures that lie ahead. They let negative emotions rule their actions and use past events to make excuses. In doing so, they become victims. As a result of their negativism—and by accepting the retirement that happens to show up—they allow their health to deteriorate and lose their zest for life.

In contrast, people with positive attitudes tend to trust their abilities to handle change and other challenges. They believe in themselves and are willing to take risks. Most people with positive attitudes also have the ability to get a grip on big issues before they become overwhelming. They seek help when it's needed, look forward rather than backward, and relish the future with a spirit of adventure. They create the retirement they want!

This is not to say that people with positive attitudes always move smoothly into a successful retirement—far from it. However, those with positive attitudes rarely play the victim. Instead, they learn from their mistakes and are not afraid to admit when they need help or advice. (They're also more apt to give help than those with negative attitudes.)

As they say in the Pike Place Fish Market in Seattle: You choose your attitude. Lest you think this concept is new and untested, these words attributed to philosopher and psychologist William James, who died in 1910, might inspire you: "The greatest discovery of my generation is that man can alter his life simply by altering his attitude of mind."

Strengthening Your Positive Attitude
You can and should strengthen your ability to be positive.

Let's take a look at how you can do that.

The first step toward developing a positive attitude is to simply make the effort whether you fully believe it's possible or not. Suspend judgment for now. Consider your effort an extended experiment if you must.

The next step is to accept reality: Your career is behind you. Don't dwell in the past, don't lament the things you didn't accomplish, don't criticize yourself for the actions you didn't take. Preventing such thoughts from becoming entrenched usually requires practice. It's also necessary to replace these thoughts with something more positive. If you find yourself slipping into negative thoughts about the past, say this to yourself: "The past is the past. What can I do now to influence my present and future?"

The more positive images, questions, and self-talk you engage in, the more positive your mindset will be. If you catch yourself drifting into a negative mindset, force yourself to refocus on the positive. Again, the key is to practice. Give your mind something positive to focus on. When you run into problems, ask yourself this question: "What do I need to do to bring about the changes I want?" Be sure to follow through on the answer(s).

People with positive attitudes see the humour in situations and can laugh at themselves. This is different from responding to situations with jaded sarcasm or by cutting yourself or others down. It might seem counterintuitive, but both of these negative responses tend to occur when we've mentally put ourselves at the centre of the universe. Volunteering, taking a walk, or watching comedy films and TV shows are some ways to lighten up.

Maintaining a positive attitude also includes believing

with conviction that you deserve love and success. If you're having trouble with this, pick up a book of affirmations and apply what you learn. Seek counselling for added guidance and support—you deserve this too!

Surrounding yourself with positive people helps as well. On the other hand, you might want to try to help people drop their own unhealthy negative attitude. Give it a try, but don't allow yourself to get stuck in the effort. Be willing to let it go if it doesn't work.

Once again, you have a choice: be negative, repel others, and look at the future with dread, or be positive, attract likeminded people, and view the future as a new and wonderful opportunity. Choose now and say your choice aloud!

Good Mental Health

I've already covered the importance of reinventing your role in life and living a balanced lifestyle. Now I'd like to touch on symptoms of distress and stress.

Upon entering retirement, you might experience butterflies, sweaty palms, upset stomach, and free-floating anxiety. First, be assured these are normal reactions to the kinds of changes associated with retirement. However, when stress builds up, your body responds to it, and it can reach overload status. Here are some possible symptoms of stress overload:

- Headaches
- Numerous colds, cold sores, and other viral disorders
- Skin rashes
- Ulcers and digestive disorders

- Irritability
- Insomnia
- Heart palpitations and high blood pressure
- Accidental injury due to inattention or distraction

As for everyday stress, you've had it before and chances are you will have it again. Just knowing retirement brings change that could cause stress is a crucial first step in learning how to cope. Taking action to reduce stress (and keep it in check) is an important next step.

As a cautionary note: If you have one or more of these symptoms, consult with your doctor.

Tips for Reducing Stress

Relaxation is one of the most powerful weapons you have to fight increased levels of stress. Here are some excellent ways to relax:

- *Physical exercise.* For many people, just the simple act of exercising is sufficient to reduce or eliminate their stress (e.g., walking, jogging, or playing tennis).

- *Deep breathing.* Take a deep breath in through your nose, hold it for ten seconds, and then release it slowly through your mouth. Repeat the process for five minutes. This can also help lower your heart rate and blood pressure.

- *Progressive muscle relaxation.* Find a comfortable place where you can stretch out and relax. This might be on a couch, in a chair, or on the floor. Shake out your arms and legs, settle back, take a deep breath, and close your eyes.

  Focus on your feet and ankles. Repeat to yourself, "My feet and ankles are relaxed, my feet and ankles are relaxed." Then concentrate on your lower legs and calves, this time repeating, "My lower legs and calves are relaxed."

  Next, concentrate on your thighs and buttocks; then your abdomen, chest, and back; then your arms and shoulders; and then your neck and head.

  This process helps many people feel completely relaxed and tension-free. You can use this progressive muscle relaxation technique every time you feel stressed, or you can use it at night to help you fall asleep.

- *Visualization.* When you feel stress and tension building, picture a place where you feel safe, happy, and comfortable. (Many people think of a sunny beach with warm temperatures and blue water lapping on the shore.)

  Once you've visualized your preferred place, take a deep breath, inhaling slowly through your nose. Hold the breath for a few seconds before exhaling through your mouth. Continue this way of breathing as you visualize your special place. See the colours of the sand, the palm trees, the sky, the ocean; smell the salty fresh air; hear the sounds of the water; feel the warm sun and the cool breeze, etc. Let the tension and stress slip away.

Combating the Blues

Even successful retirees and people who are normally positive get the blues. Below is a partial list of the most common things that get people down as well as suggestions for pulling yourself back up. See "Combating the Blues" in Part II for a full list with suggestions.

1. Feeling the holiday blues
   - If you often feel blue during holidays, make plans to do something well in advance. Trying to make last-minute plans might cause you to feel worse.
   - Invite a friend to do something with you (rather than wait to be invited).
   - Volunteer at a shelter, volunteer to deliver meals, or volunteer to help with an activity that happens during the holidays. Many charities have holiday themed events that succeed only with help from the community.
   - Go see a movie on the biggest day of the holiday (e.g., Christmas Day or Thanksgiving Day). Seeing a comedy might be particularly helpful.

2. Dreading weekends
   - Increase your weekend activities, including physical exercise.
   - Make plans to do something with friends in advance.

3. Experiencing the winter blues
   - Engage in winter-specific activities such as skating or skiing.
   - Look into light therapy (or phototherapy).

- Speak to your doctor about seasonal affective disorder (SAD).

4. Feeling lethargic, sleeping too much, experiencing insomnia, or sleeping during the day and being awake at night
- Get more physical exercise, including taking regular walks.
- Add a short afternoon nap to your regular routine, but don't nap for longer than thirty minutes, as this could disrupt your sleep schedule.
- Don't watch TV or use electronics such as a computer or smartphone within an hour of your bedtime. The light from the screens can disrupt your sleep schedule.
- See your doctor and get a physical. Ask for advice on how to improve your sleep quality.

5. Feeling sorry for yourself and/or resenting others
- Watch a comedy.
- Watch a sad movie and have what my wife tells me is a "good" cry.
- Listen to your favourite upbeat and cheerful music. Also consider listening to sad music. Much like watching sad movies, listening to sad music allows us to experience sympathetic emotions.
- Make an effort to identify the positives in life (also known as counting your blessings).
- Volunteer to help others or visit someone who is ill or hospitalized.

It's important to pay attention to your moods. If you find

that you feel down for an extended period and that various symptoms keep nagging you, be sure discuss with your doctor the possibility that you might suffer from depression. Left untreated, depression can entrench itself and even spiral out of control, making it that much harder to overcome. The sooner you get a diagnosis and start treatment, the better.

More on Stress and the Blues

There are two other things I want to suggest as stress relievers: 1) talk things out and/or ask for help, and 2) slow changes down.

Remember that you need not handle things alone. We need—and should not be afraid to ask for—sympathy, understanding, knowledge, and encouragement from friends, family, and professionals such as therapists. Share your concerns and ask for their thoughts and suggestions on how to handle the situation.

Making the transition from work to retirement often involves sharp and abrupt changes. If you find yourself feeling very stressed, consider slowing additional changes down or making smaller changes when possible. This does not mean you should put your planning and implementation aside completely. The more active you are in choosing and determining changes, the more satisfied you'll be in retirement. Activity, in turn, tends to help generate a more positive outlook. The important thing is to pay attention to your stress levels and adjust accordingly.

Keeping Your Brain Stimulated

Good mental health includes keeping our brain active and

challenged. As we age, we need to pay extra attention to keeping our brain cells working! Here are some tips for engaging your brain cells and increasing your general mental health:

- Work on brainteasers, logic problems, word games, and puzzles.
- Play board games that require strategic thinking, such as chess and checkers.
- Do math without a calculator.
- Use your non-dominant hand for activities such as brushing your teeth or moving a computer mouse.
- Visualize, spell, pronounce, and write words backwards.
- Take up juggling.
- Attend debates and lectures.
- Take classes, including online classes.
- Participate in Toastmasters, an international club for helping people improve their communication skills.
- Teach classes, run workshops, and give talks on an area of interest or expertise.
- Learn to play a musical instrument.
- Memorize lists, songs, and poems.
- Learn a foreign language.
- Read a book or magazine instead of watching TV. If you're already an avid reader, try reading material that is challenging instead of simply entertaining.
- Play 3-D video games to develop and maintain your brain's spatial navigation and memory formation capacities. Video games aren't just for kids anymore.

A note of caution: Items marketed to keep our brains healthy abound. Stay away from "miracle" products and services

costing hundreds of dollars or promising results that are un-
verified by credible third parties. In addition, consult with
your doctor before taking herbs or other supplements.

Spirituality

As part of our mental health toolbox, we also have spirituality in its many forms. Older adults are more likely to
encounter difficult life events such as the death of a friend
or partner, or the diagnosis of a serious disease. Spiritual
and religious practices give us coping patterns and skills
to deal with what life throws our way.

Spirituality can certainly provide comfort in difficult
times, but there's more to it than that. It also helps many
people appreciate and enjoy the life they lead, including
their life in retirement. In fact, studies completed for
groups such as the National Interfaith Coalition on Aging
(NICA) in the U.S. have related happiness, high morale,
and good health to spirituality. The opposite was also
found: People with less spirituality are generally not as
happy or healthy as those with a high degree of spirituality.

Take steps to increase your spirituality, whether in a
house of worship, in reflection or meditation, in appreciation of nature in parks and in your front yard, or in the
sound of someone's laughter.

If spirituality is something new to you, consider reading one of the many introductory books available, or even
pay a visit to a local religious centre or meditation class.
Most of them are welcoming to visitors and willing to introduce them to their spiritual practices.

Using Visualization for Mental Health and Spirituality
Visualization is a powerful tool for a successful retirement. Visualizing yourself in a safe, relaxing place is one way to reduce stress. Visualization is also often used in meditation and prayer.

Our ability to plan for a successful retirement is also very much linked to our ability to visualize. Visualizing a satisfying and well-balanced retirement is the key to setting goals and then going after them. Being able to visualize also makes it easier to communicate with those who can help you achieve your vision. This can include your partner, your friends, and your financial advisor.

Some people find it easy to visualize in great detail. Others...well, let me assure you it's not uncommon for the "wrong" thing to pop into our heads. Fortunately, visualization is indeed a skill you can learn or strengthen.

Take a look at the comments below. Those unfamiliar with visualization might think that the first one represents an excellent visualization and that the second one doesn't.

I envision myself continuing in my profession but only working two days a week. My wife and I are having fun together, attending auctions, concerts, and travelling. I am spending approximately one day a week doing volunteer work. I see myself swimming at the local indoor pool twice a week and golfing once a week in the spring and summer. I am eating healthy meals and even cooking those meals regularly. I also envision my wife and me spending about 20 percent of our time with our children and grandchildren, simply enjoying each other's com-

pany as well as special events as our treat.
—Raymond P., college professor

You mentioned having a retirement vision several times. At one point, you even invited us to close our eyes and picture something. That was a nice relaxing moment. But I have to confess all I managed to picture was the kitchen sink, which happens to be full of dishes right now.
—Heather M., chiropractor

In truth, there is no "good" or "bad" visualization, especially since the process is often more important than the images themselves. Should you choose to develop this skill—and I encourage you to do so—your goal is not necessarily to emulate the first example above. The art of visualization is as individual as you are. The dos and don'ts below will help you get started.

Things to avoid:

- Don't try to force a crystal-clear, fully detailed picture, or one that makes complete sense. Our mental images are rarely like those in movies. Simply let the images flow.

- Don't try to force yourself to fill in all of the mental blanks. For example, it's fine to imagine a new home even if you can't quite picture the living room or where the home is.

- Don't be alarmed at the number of blanks or gaps either because it's quite common to have quite a few. Let these go for now. If desired, focus on one blank or gap at another time, visualizing it by itself.

- Don't go overboard: visualize within your means and be practical.

Things to do:

- Pay attention to the positive images that come easily to mind. You can build on these, but try not to be alarmed if you have more negative images and feelings than positive ones. This is fairly common. In fact, I encourage you to make note of these negative images.

- One of the hallmarks of an unsuccessful retirement is a habit of turning away from fears and concerns. Unsuccessful retirees not only fail to plan; they also often pull the mental covers up over their head. It's easy to understand how this happens. For example, a man once told me that when picturing moving to a different home, all he could think of was the chore of wading through years of accumulated stuff in the garage. Thinking about the task—and the probable arguments with his wife over keeping, tossing, or donating things—was overwhelming. He gave up even though his current home was not satisfactory. Unfortunately, this choice helped generate rather serious repercussions in later years.

As strange as it sounds, negative pictures,

thoughts, and feelings are building blocks for your retirement vision. Successful retirees face their fears and get help to overcome challenges.

- Focus on the rewards of a balanced retirement. Throughout the retirement visioning process, it is imperative to be optimistic about your future. Enjoy feeling complete, being enriched and financially secure. Nurture the positive parts of your vision by actively and proactively calling them to mind. In other words, practice picturing positive things. This practice will make strong positive images come more easily.

  Notice that I said to practice imagining the *positive* portions of your vision. Don't let yourself dwell on fears and negatives because that will make them stronger too. To shake any negative images off, open your eyes (if they were closed) and move from where you are sitting or lying. In other words, get up and walk about for a bit.

- Try to come up with a mental image for every aspect of your retirement. The goal is to imagine where you live, what you do with your time, etc. This is not to say that you'll have a cohesive vision or something that runs along a linear path. Visualizing in pieces works just as well.

If you haven't yet retired or are newly retired, it might be helpful to visualize a successful retirement in time increments. Imagine yourself specifically in your first six months of retirement, and then imagine yourself in one year, and then again in two years. Does the mental picture change? If so, how?

Although this visualization is intended to clarify your retirement plan, it's advisable to revisit your vision throughout retirement. This can help you identify changes you need to make and help you move forward to plan and implement the next steps.

Using Pictures with Visualization

Drawing has long been used as a tool to improve visualization. Such drawings might not be the kind you frame and hang on the wall, and that's quite all right. Once again, the process is often far more important.

If you don't enjoy drawing, you might find it helpful to create a collage of images. Magazines are a good resource, as are some of your own personal photos. Your collage might cover your entire retirement vision, or just some parts of it, such as your home or how you'll spend your time.

Whether you use drawings or collages, the end result is a mental vision that has become something concrete. This might help you develop your vision into reality.

Non-Visual Visualization

Everyone's brain works a bit differently, and some people, including but not exclusively many who are blind, do not imagine pictures. Instead, other sensory "images" and feelings come to mind. For example, someone imagining the colour green or a lawn might have a sense of coolness and what the grass feels like. Someone visualizing a comfortable home might experience a tactile or kinetic sense of comfortably moving through the rooms.

If you experience something similar as you practice visualization, go with it. Don't force yourself to try to picture things, especially if the effort becomes frustrating. Experiment, and then practice what occurs most easily.

Writing and Visualization

Many people find that writing helps clarify their retirement vision and that it has a positive effect on attitude and mental health.

The writing process helps clarify thoughts, wants, concerns, and needs, and it also encourages a goal-directed approach. For example, if you identify "being physically fit" as an important need, you should include appropriate measures to ensure that this need is met in your retirement plan.

What are your thoughts, wants, concerns, and needs? You might want to take a few minutes to jot down your thoughts. Here is an example list to get you going:

I have a need or want to:
- Give and receive kindness, enjoy companionship
- Get involved in interesting and thought-provoking endeavours
- Become a respected authority in my favourite hobby
- Have time for and meaningful relationships with loved ones
- Be physically and mentally fit
- Be financially secure
- Enjoy life, have fun
- Help others, contributing to their well-being

- Possess inner harmony and peace, living by my beliefs

Should you write things down? Some find it helpful, some don't. Some people keep a journal to jot down images, concerns, ideas, and questions. They essentially process things on paper to help themselves process things mentally. Even if keeping a journal is not your style, I encourage you to write down questions and make notes about things you need help with. With the help of others, you can use these notes as a springboard for brainstorming ideas and solutions.

Chapter 7
Strategies for Success

In speaking with retirees, it's clear to me that those who create and maintain a successful retirement consistently apply certain strategies. Some retirees weren't particularly aware that they were applying any strategies, but when I analyzed what helps them succeed, the commonalities were striking.

These strategies are outlined below. Use this information in your self-assessments, which you will get to later in this book. Where you have current strengths, be sure to continue to apply them in developing and maintaining a successful retirement. Where you discover gaps or areas needing work, use this information to apply these strategies and strengthen your ability to succeed.

The strategies for success are:

1. Use the concept of legacy to guide your actions
2. Proactively enhance relationships
3. Improve communication
4. Plan and stick to a budget
5. Organize papers and research services before needing them
6. Work with mentors
7. Write things down

Strategy 1: Use the Concept of Legacy to Guide Your Actions

Successful retirees give considerable thought to how they want to be remembered. This is not an exercise in conceit; it's a way to clarify what is important to you.

Legacy is not just money you pass on to your heirs. Legacy is about life and living. It's about learning from the past, living in the present, and building for the future. If you don't pass on your life experience by leaving a legacy, the wisdom you've gained through decades of difficult learning will be lost. A legacy can take many forms: children, grandchildren, a business, record of family ancestry, cherished memories, valued lessons, etc. Hopefully, your life experiences and accomplishments will help those who remain to both remember you and learn from your time on this earth.

Strategy 2: Proactively Build and Enhance Relationships

Humans are social beings, and retirement is the time when you most need companionship—and you often have to work harder to ensure you have it.

To be successful socially, you need to work at keeping up with current friends and be proactive in seeking new ones. This means continually going to social events and gatherings, meeting people, and sending out positive signals of interest. Each of us needs to keep adding people to our list of acquaintances, and in time some might join our circle of close friends.

Strategy 3: Improve Communication

Improving your communication skills helps improve your relationship with your partner as well as your relationships with other people who are significant in your life.

In retirement, the relationship that often changes is the one with your partner. Due to hectic lives, the average married couple spends only three hours a week together without the children. In today's world, communication lines are becoming stretched and broken. However, a relationship filled with good times isn't something that just happens. Like all aspects of retirement, it requires planning and effort. This includes ensuring your partner feels valued, appreciated, and loved.

Strategy 4: Plan and Stick to a Budget

Successful retirees endorse calculating and keeping a budget. Many also report they had to learn or relearn the process.

No matter where you're living or what you plan to do in retirement, you probably want to maintain your present standard of living. To assist you in this process, personal budgeting is critical. Budgeting helps you determine where your money comes from, where it goes, and how much is left over at the end of the month. It provides you with a clear picture of what your current lifestyle is costing you.

Strategy 5: Organize Papers and Research Services Before Needing Them

Personal disorganization is a trap and a time waster. It can cause frustration and feelings of resentment for those who have to "pick up the pieces" if you become injured, seriously ill, or deceased.

Successful retirees report that organizing their personal papers such as their will and insurance policies; listing their credit card and bank accounts; creating a list of people to be notified about injury, illness, or death; recording their thoughts on funeral arrangements, etc., provides them with a sense of control and peace. This book includes some simple steps you can take that will benefit you and your loved ones tremendously.

Strategy 6: Work with Mentors
A little guidance can go a long way, including in a successful retirement. Now you're entering one of the most challenging yet exciting times of your life. Retirement is filled with adventure, change, and the unknown. Faced with this new part of your life, you can choose to jump into retirement with both feet, without any planning or discussion, or you can enter retirement fully prepared. As part of your retirement preparation, consider finding and using one or more mentors to provide you with the advice and emotional support you'll need to be a successful retiree.

Strategy 7: Write Things Down
We live in a fast-paced world with tremendous convenience, and we love to get things done quickly. We have little time to think about what we have done and how we did it. However, if we are to be successful in our retirement life, we need to take time to reflect on our actions to see what worked, see what could have been done differently, and plan for our next challenges. Writing things down (journaling) is a way to slow down and help us assess where we've been and where we're going.

Chapter 8

Imagine Your Legacy —
Success Strategy 1

Successful retirees give considerable thought to how they want to be remembered. They suggest imagining being ninety, ninety-five, or a hundred years old. In old age, when you look back on your life, what will stand out as your best accomplishments? When others think of you, what will their memories be?

This is not an exercise in conceit; rather, it can help you identify what's truly important in your life. This is part of what's needed to imagine, plan, implement, and maintain a successful retirement. Take the following description, for example:

> *I want to be remembered as a fabulous granddad.*
> *I try my best to attend most of my grandson's and*
> *granddaughter's sporting events. I help out at their*
> *school. I take them to the zoo, play with them in*
> *the yard, and join them on campouts.*
> —Harry B., industrial engineer

At first glance, Harry's desire to be remembered as a wonderful grandfather might seem rather commonplace. Upon closer analysis, however, you'll recognize how his concept of legacy has helped him build a balanced leisure lifestyle:

- He keeps physically active by playing with his grand-children and by hiking during campouts.
- He nurtures his social circle in part by volunteering at his grandchildren's school.
- His trips to the zoo and attending sporting events provide entertainment.
- Spending time with his grandchildren nurtures his relationships with them, and it might also enhance his relationships with their parents—his own children.

The following is another example of how a concept of legacy prompted someone to take certain actions:

Many years after I am gone, I'd like my love for animals to live on. My financial planner knows this and has helped me identify certain assets to give to my favourite shelter after I have passed. It won't matter that those assets are not nearly enough to put my name on a building. And in the meantime, I give my time at the shelter three days a week, teaching new volunteers.
—Elsa T., former newspaper journalist

Elsa'a love for animals has current benefits for her as well:

- She worked with her financial advisor on what amounts to an estate plan.
- She has a social circle of friends who work and volunteer at the animal shelter.
- Volunteering adds structure and a sense of fulfillment to her life.

- Teaching volunteers continually broadens her social circle and helps keep her brain challenged and healthy.

Legacies can be big or small. The key is to ask yourself, "How do I want to be remembered?" This question helps you keep perspective and will guide you in setting priorities for taking action.

Other Ways to Use Legacy

How many times have you wondered about your ancestors? This kind of curiosity is something likely shared by many in your family. Another way to build on your concept of legacy is to leave a gift of family history to the ones you love.

Where did your family originate? Who were your great-grandparents? Are you related to pioneers, a famous explorer, or a revolutionary scientist? Were your relations all commoners, or were some of them members of the gentry or nobility? Their lives probably still hold great fascination for younger generations, and it's not necessary to have all the details.

My grandkids are amazed at the kinds of work my grandfather did. Lead miner. Piano player. He worked in the first avocado orchards in California, and then the shipyards in World War II. These jobs seem exotic, and we enjoy talking about what that life may have been like.
—Paulo S., ship's captain

Now is the time to record your knowledge about yourself and your mother, father, siblings, aunts, uncles, cousins, and other family members. Make the effort to record where you and the others were born, and list any insights into who everyone is and was, including occupations, personality traits, experiences and adventures, hobbies and interests, etc. As part of this wonderful gesture, also list information about your family's medical history. These facts will be useful and possibly even lifesaving to your children and grandchildren.

It's amazing how much information we can collect about our families and how deeply this information will be treasured. Here are some items to consider recording as a living memory for your loved ones:

- A descriptive list of your values, beliefs, and thoughts about your faith.
- Things you learned from your grandparents, parents, partner, and children; and things you learned from others such as friends, mentors, heroes, etc.
- Things you are grateful for and your hopes for the future.
- Important events and accomplishments in your life and the lives of your relatives.
- Things you regret not doing and the lessons learned along the way.
- Your happiest times.
- Your most memorable projects, events, etc.
- Stories about your children when they were young (grandchildren especially enjoy these).

You might also consider a narrative approach, writing

stories that illustrate what life was like. Share specifics or tidbits as you can. What was the hourly wage for your first job? How much did your first car cost? What was the make and model, and what were its exciting "new" features? This kind of historical context might even be something people beyond family will enjoy. If you believe so, consider writing a full memoir; in fact, memoir-writing classes are very popular at senior centres.

Keep in mind that writing is not the only mode to consider. Audio and video recordings are just as wonderful, if not more. We now have easy access to digital recording (even with our phones). You might even find that making such recordings is easier than writing about certain subjects.

Remember, too, that researching, organizing your thoughts, writing, recording, and taking classes for any purpose help you lead a balanced and successful retired life.

Leaving a Legacy Isn't a Competition

After giving a talk on successful retirement, it's not uncommon for people to comment about my own apparent legacy. Most see my work as an author and speaker as being a part of my desired legacy (it is); however, everything is not necessarily as it seems.

Since I'm constantly in the public eye, some people think their own legacies would seem small or unimportant compared to mine. This is quite flattering and a bit worrisome at the same time. Don't let comparing yourself to others discourage you from applying your own strategy of creating your legacy. Each person's legacy can be truly large. Even the smallest act, contribution, or memory can leave a lasting impact on others—including those far beyond your immediate family or circle of friends—often in ways you're unaware of.

What's more, like most people, my personal work on legacy began quite modestly. That it grew substantially isn't what makes it worthwhile; rather, the effort itself is what makes it worthwhile. I enjoy the fulfillment I get from helping people achieve a successful retirement, whether through my writing, my speaking, or the one-on-one chats I have with those I meet while out walking.

Finally, my concept of legacy is not solely focused on the work I do as an author and speaker. I also wish to be remembered as someone who explored the world as much possible as a loving husband and as a supportive father and grandfather. These elements of legacy guide my actions.

Chapter 9
Proactively Build and Enhance Relationships—Success Strategy 2

Humans are social beings. We feel most comfortable when surrounded by those with whom we share mutual feelings of love, trust, and understanding. We also feel energized when relating to people who share our interests—as well as those who challenge our thinking and broaden our horizons!

Retirement is the time when you most need companionship, and you might need to work harder to ensure you have it. There are several ways to help you foster strong relationships.

Relationships with Co-Workers and Colleagues

Most people realize that the relationships they have with people at work will change drastically or become a distant memory when they retire. Many people stay in touch in the beginning, but as months pass, the contact tends to dwindle. Eventually, if left to chance, there will be occasional thoughts of people but little or no interaction with them.

The principal [of the school where I had worked]
contacted me to ask if I'd work with some of the
new teachers. Returning to campus made me real-
ize how much I missed a few people in particular.
From that point on, I made a point to ask them for

coffee or dinner every now and then.
—Alice W., former teacher

You need to forge a new path in retirement: let go of some relationships and build new ones. If you want to stay in contact with workplace buddies, don't wait for them to contact you; give them a call! However, remember that they're still very busy with work. Ask if they can meet you for lunch or a quick coffee. Don't take it personally if they need to postpone or cancel. Persist and reschedule, but also be prepared to let it go.

Making New Friends

A successful retirement includes making new friends. You'll most likely need to be proactive in this.

If, for example, you meet people at a memoir-writing class or at the local coffee shop, strike up a conversation. Inquire about the other person, asking open-ended questions about their interests and life, and be sure to listen to their answers intently. Also be sure to share details about your own interests and life. Remember that it helps to discover mutual interests and experiences. From there, extend an invitation to do something together, such as seeing a movie, visiting a new museum exhibit, or meeting at the driving range for a bucket and a beer.

My neighbour and I had a nodding acquaintance. We'd exchange a few words of commiseration over the amount of snow on our walks, that kind of thing. One day, I realized neither of us was working. I invited him over to watch the game, which

became a weekly thing. Some time later, he invited me down to his [Grand] Lodge. Things "snow-balled" from there, and I became a lodge member.
—Russell I., bricklayer

Whatever you do, make the effort to continually meet new people. Keep adding people to your list of acquaintances. In time, some might join your circle of close friends.

Expressing Appreciation

Cy, a former carpenter, constantly expresses appreciation to those in his social circle, including sending birthday cards to his financial advisor, accountant, and insurance agent. When asked why he makes the effort, his answer is, "These people are important to me. They play a critical role in my life and help me keep my financial and personal affairs in order."

Cy's perspective holds good advice for us all. As part of your relationship development, think about how you can express appreciation for the people important enough to be in your social circle. In addition to your partner, family members, and close friends, give serious consideration to acknowledging your spiritual leader, doctor, dentist, insurance agent, financial advisor, accountant, lawyer, and neighbours.

Here's why the above individuals deserve some acknowledgment: Your spiritual leader provides you with guidance; your doctor, dentist, insurance agent, financial advisor, accountant, and lawyer provide their professional services and advice; and your neighbours provide peace of mind when you're away and camaraderie when you're home. In short, each of these people provides you with something important. Take the time to go above and beyond mere reciprocation—let those in your circle know how much they mean to you.

Recognizing people for playing an important role in your life is a very personal gesture, and how you do it will vary from person to person, relationship to relationship. It might be as simple as offering a heartfelt thank you to let them know your feelings and how you appreciate their contributions.

Here are other ideas from retirees who have made a point of showing their appreciation and then enjoyed better relationships as a result:

My CPA is crazy-busy during tax season. I make a point of giving her a call every couple weeks around 11:00 and offering to bring her lunch. Only costs me a few dollars, and it's enjoyable to visit with her and give to her, considering all the free advice she's given my family members over the years.
—Nella F., former railway supervisor

Of course, I tip the person who cuts my hair. I also send her a birthday card, which she likes so much it stays posted on her station for months.
—Hans R., sculptor

My neighbour often pulls the garbage and recycling bins up into my driveway after the trucks have come around. I make a point of knocking on his door and telling him thank you. He always gruffly says, "They were in the street," but I can tell he's tickled to be thanked.

—Albert S., chartered accountant

We have the kind of grocery store in which bagging clerks regularly offer to help us out to the car. These kids help out no matter how cold, windy, or rainy it is. We're not allowed to tip them, so it took me a little while to figure out how to express my appreciation. I made a point of learning their names, and then I wrote to their supervisor about what a great job they each do.

—Carmella X., music teacher

Enhancing Your Relationship with Your Partner

Upon your retirement, your relationship with your partner is most likely the relationship that will change the most. The same is generally true of the relationships for many people who share a home, and so the suggestions below also apply to people beyond partners.

My sister and I have shared a home for years. Though we technically have separate residences, we shared child-rearing tasks and still share most chores, split expenses, and have many meals together. When she retired, we found ourselves bickering quite a bit, which we had not done since purchasing the home and dividing the chores many years prior.

—Yon J., gardener

The change can be particularly striking when retirement occurs soon after the children have left the "nest." A survey published by the University of Minnesota in December 2013, "Time for Each Other: Work and Family Constraints Among Couples," found that the average couple with children living at home spends only three or four hours a week together (without the children). Although the study didn't look into it, it's likely those three or four hours a week are spent collapsing on the couch and watching TV.

Even when there haven't been children in the home for years (or at all), the amount and nature of time spent together changes. Before retirement, each person tends to have developed a schedule and routine around work, family, friends, and home. When retirement comes, it affects much of that.

Make a Plan and Make the Effort

Retirement is a time to relax and enjoy the fruits of your labour, which includes spending quality time with your partner. It's supposed to be the time to enrich your relationship, to do things and go places together. However, a relationship filled with good times isn't something that just happens. Like all other aspects of retirement, it requires planning and effort.

As part of your holistic plan, it's important to recognize that you and your partner have each built up your own space and privacy needs. You both need time for your own interests, hobbies, and tasks, or just to "chill out" alone. Be sure to discuss your individual needs with each other and to come to an agreement on how they can be met. The following guideline might be helpful for your discussions: If you were apart from your partner eight hours a day during your working days, plan to be apart approximately four hours a day in retirement. This gives both of you your own time and space.

As a couple, it's also important to discuss what retirement means to both of you in terms of roles and responsibilities. You might find it's also time to reinvent how your roles interact. Discuss things such as:

1. *Who does what around the house?* Will one of you now do more or less of the grocery shopping, cooking, or other chores? Also discuss how new interests might affect the other person. Just because you now have more time to cook gourmet meals doesn't mean your partner will be happy to clean up the mess.

2. *Schedules and coordination.* Will you generally be home for dinner at a certain time? Should you inform your partner about any new activities that might affect your usual routines? Are there old activities you intend to continue?

When my wife retired, she expected me to stop hanging out with my buddies at the local watering hole. I had no idea that was her expectation. All I knew was that when I came home for dinner after shooting the bull for a couple hours, just like I'd done for the last twenty years, she was fuming about something. It finally blew up, and that's when it all came out.
—Hank G., former warehouse supervisor

3. *Your household budget.* Many couples have never had a budget discussion up to this point. Don't let that deter you from regularly discussing monthly budgets. Be sure to ask the important questions. Is your monthly income now more limited? Are expenses reduced since you no longer commute to work or maintain an expensive work wardrobe? Do you want to save for something? Do you need to adjust how much you spend on groceries? Do you need to budget for new pursuits, such as cooking classes or a health club membership?

   Ever since my husband retired, I worry over every little expense. Can we still afford this magazine subscription? Can I buy those shoes, or should I ask him about it first? Should I buy milk instead of half-and-half? Your talk has inspired me to discuss budgeting with him.
   —Emma Y., store clerk

4. *What and/or where is each person's "territory"?* Our workplace often provides personal territory, and this changes with retirement. You might need to identify or create a new personal space or territory at home, possibly for each of you.

   Be aware that more time on your hands can lead to accidental encroachment. Your retirement isn't necessarily a good opportunity to "organize" your partner's workbench in the garage. Talk about it before you take action.

I was still working when my husband, a project manager, retired. While I was at work, he reorganized the kitchen cupboards even though he did not cook. That was problem one. He then rearranged the living room furniture to accommodate a very large TV he purchased without discussing it with me. The proverbial icing was when he signed us both up for courses at the senior centre, again without discussing it. By then I was furious, and we actually stopped speaking for several days.

—Cathy O., former tax specialist

5. *Doing things together, whether or not both of you are retired.* Couples who have shared interests and activities aside from home and children are generally far happier. If you don't currently have such shared activities, make the effort to find some. Brainstorm a list of possibilities, create a plan to test-drive, and then follow through. Some couples actually create a written description or agreement, potentially including an outline of dates, duties, responsibilities, and authorities.

   For example, when Frank retired from his job as a construction manager, he and his wife, Amber, created a written agreement. Frank would participate in activities outside the home three mornings a week. While Amber had the house to herself, she would enjoy her hobby, which was pottery. The couple agreed to walk to their favourite pastry shop for coffee twice a week and have a date night every Thursday. They also reset the kitchen duties, specifying who was to shop, cook, do the dishes, take out the garbage, etc.

Whether decisions or agreements are expressed on paper or not, discussing how your roles and activities interact will help prevent problems.

Express Appreciation

Essential elements of a happy relationship include feeling valued, appreciated, and loved. When a couple lacks any one of these, the relationship suffers and the partners drift apart. Simply spending more time together (as in retirement) can exacerbate these problems.

Preparation for a successful retirement provides you with an opportunity to assess and enhance your relationship. Try beginning with reinforcing your appreciation of your partner as well as friends and family members dear to you. Take the time to self-assess the following:

- Are you thoughtful?
- Do you have a sense of fun and adventure?
- Do you express appreciation clearly and unambiguously?

The above traits, among others, add to the quality of your relationship and the satisfaction level between you and your partner. It could be as simple as saying thank you to recognize what your partner does for you and your relationship.

To add spice to your relationship, do things such as buy flowers or treat your partner to a romantic dinner.

Similar actions of a less romantic nature help freshen relationships with friends and family members as well. Purchase a book you think your brother-in-law will enjoy;

take your good friend to his favourite restaurant and pick up the bill; drop your daughter a note telling her how proud you are of her.

It's also extremely important to spend quality time with people and share fun activities. Relationships are like a garden; they require regular care and feeding!

Take time to reflect privately as well. Consider whether feeling comfortable with your loved one has also made you a bit lazy. When was the last time you cleared the dishes or made your partner's favourite dish? Do you regularly ask about their day? Do you notice what your partner is doing, engage them in conversation, ask for their opinion? These are the kinds of things we do early on in the relationship, but they tend to drop away as time goes on. Unfortunately, the message isn't so much that we feel very comfortable but more that we take our loved one for granted.

If you tend to be indifferent about your appearance, start making an effort to look good—not only when you're going out but also when lounging around the house. This, too, sends a positive message to your partner (it also tends to improve your own attitude). However, before you make such changes, you should let your partner know of your intentions. Communication is, as always, important.

My wife and I have a relationship our children say is old-fashioned. She stayed home and ran our household, and I was the breadwinner. Some months after I retired, I began to notice she no longer wore her comfy sweatpants around the house unless she was gardening. I then realized she frequently wore a bit of makeup. She also smiled more often and had a bit of a glow about her. Imagine my relief when I found notes she'd taken at [one of your talks] indicating a commit-ment to look nice for me!

—José E., former baseball manager

Chapter 10
Improve Communication— Success Strategy 3

Between reading this book and living your life experiences, you have probably noticed that many problems are created by poor communication or a lack of communication. The reverse is also true: Good communication is vital for a successful retirement when you are part of a couple.

For many couples, retirement comes as quite a shock. Both partners have been wrapped up in their world of work, possibly taking care of the kids and maintaining the home for years, which leaves little time for each other. Then comes retirement, and then there is just the two of them!

Extra time together means your patterns of communication—even good communication—might get shaken up. What's more, if one or both of you feel you've been misunderstood, weren't listened to, or were treated with less than adequate respect, then spending more time together will tend to exacerbate that strain to the relationship.

The old patterns or methods of communication might not be as effective anymore, in part because you both have less space to cool off—less time to let mountains return to their true molehill size. Such stressors call for new communication behaviour.

Don't fall into the trap of believing that everything must be okay if your partner isn't complaining, nor should you self-sabotage your happiness with the idea that your wants and needs should be obvious. Open the lines of communication and encourage discussion about each other's concerns with the mindset of finding solutions, agreements, and acceptable compromises.

Assess Your Communication Skills

Assessing how you currently communicate with your partner should be a part of your retirement planning. It will help you determine if changes are needed. Although it might be tempting to focus this assessment on your partner's "failings," you'll be far more successful if you focus on yourself. In fact, changing how *you* communicate often has the quickest positive impact on how your partner communicates with you.

Although by no means is this a comprehensive list, the following questions can help you begin your self-assessment:

- Do I let things slide for too long, only to bring them up when I'm also feeling upset about it?
- Do I tune out when my partner says something I don't agree with or don't want to hear?
- Do I listen primarily to what I want to hear or feared I'd hear?
- Do I interrupt while my partner is talking?
- Do I form a rebuttal in my head while my partner is talking?
- Do I assume I already know what my partner is going to say?
- Do I clearly acknowledge my partner's point of view, opinion, wants, needs, etc.?

It might also be helpful to identify the positives, this time in terms of your partner. For example:

- I know my partner is listening when....
- My partner values what I think or have to say by....
- One of our communication strengths is....

Also take some time to identify any hot-button issues. Are there any topics that tend to create argument? Think of any other topics you avoid for some reason, including to avoid an argument.

You and your partner can complete your self-assessments separately and then discuss the results to help improve your communication. Regardless of whether your partner participates, you can use what you've learned as a springboard.

Tips for Improving Communication

The following is a list of tips that will help you improve the communication in your relationship. Try to keep them in mind whenever you interact with your partner.

1. *Think your message through in advance.* We've all said things we regret. A little forethought, and choosing words more carefully, can help you get your message across in the best way possible.

   For example, "You don't know what you're talking about" is bound to ruffle some feathers. "I hear what you're saying, and I have a different view" would likely be better received. Instead of saying, "This food is terrible!" try, "This doesn't taste quite right to me. How does it taste to you?" (Or word it the other way around.)

If you don't feel a discussion is progressing, avoid statements such as "Let's just drop it" because they tend to generate resentment for both parties. Instead, try something along the lines of "I'd like to take a break. Would it be okay with you if we leave this for an hour or two?" (Although a day or two might be even better.)

2. *Choose a good time (or at least avoid choosing a bad time)*. Ask your partner if now is a good time for you to talk. If it's not, negotiate for one that is. Avoid asking for discussion at a time you know your partner won't appreciate (e.g., while the game is on, when they're walking out the door to go to work, when they've just arrived home from work, etc.).

Choose a good time for yourself too. On the one hand, accumulating small resentments or choosing to talk about something "little" when you've had a stressful day can make mountains out of molehills. On the other hand, letting things go for a while can provide valuable perspective, sometimes also taking the heat out of a topic.

3. *Give your partner your full attention*. Not only does giving your full attention increase your comprehension; it also shows that you care about what your partner has to say. Stop what you're doing and listen. Turn off the TV, put down the newspaper, and make eye contact.

Don't listen just to be polite; listen to understand.

Hear your partner's words and tone, and read their body language. Ask questions for clarification.

4. *Try to understand and express your partner's point of view.* Try to see the world through your partner's eyes. When you think you understand what they're saying, summarize your understanding and ask if you're correct: "What I think I'm hearing is.... Is that right?" This gives you important clarity and can help you avoid responding in a defensive tone.

5. *Practice acceptance of your partner's vulnerabilities and understand what your own hot buttons are.* In most cases, we didn't create any vulnerability in our partner—or visa versa. Nonetheless, we have to deal with our partner's hot button, and they have to deal with ours. The following is a situation that demonstrates this.

When arguments became heated, Jake's wife, Penny, often angrily complained that he was acting as if she were "stupid." Feeling unfairly accused and unable to "get anywhere" in resolving the original issue, Jake would eventually storm out of the house, ostensibly to cool off—as his father would do long ago.

After taking the self-assessment, Jake realized he sometimes didn't acknowledge what Penny said. He also realized stomping out of the house wasn't the right thing to do. Jake worked on his own communication first, taking care to show Penny he was listening and cared about what she had to say. This worked wonders.

Communication is a two-way street of expressing yourself and letting others have their say, showing respect and being respected, and truly listening and being heard. When it comes to your partner, the stakes are even higher, which is one reason why making the effort to improve is so valuable.

Again, most of this strategy for success applies to all of our close relationships, including those we have with our children and dear friends. Improving communication with these individuals also has many benefits.

Regularly revisit your communication successes and gauge your progress. Over time, you will notice your areas of strength rising, the items you need to change diminishing, and your relationships certainly improving.

Chapter 11

Plan and Stick to a Budget— Success Strategy 4

If you're not yet retired, a well-prepared monthly budget provides a clear picture of what your current lifestyle costs. You and your advisors need this information to determine when you can retire, how long your funds should last, whether you will need to make changes, etc.

When you're retired, setting and adhering to a budget is the simplest way to maintain healthy finances. In fact, successful retirees are unanimous in their endorsement of calculating and keeping a personal budget.

In contrast, the hazards involved with not setting and working within a budget can be quite serious. The problems often also affect a retiree's loved ones, as the following situation demonstrates.

Larry, an executive with an electronics firm and Eva, a photographer, looked forward to retirement—time to enjoy, relax, and savour time together. Although they had built up a nice nest egg, Larry began dipping heavily into their cash to support his hobby of restoring old cars. Soon, the nest egg shrank drastically. Larry reassured Eva that all would be well when he sold two or more of his "beauties." It's been four years of restoring and spending, and there hasn't been a single sold sign. Eva wakes up at night worried that Larry might be spending them out of their home.

Working with a budget does not necessarily mean you have to deny yourself, but it might mean you have to make adjustments. Making adjustments can be difficult and perhaps downright painful; however, once the right adjustments are made, the feeling of ease is priceless.

I've always set and stuck with a budget as much as possible. Doesn't mean I'm tight with a nickel or suffering, just means I do the math and don't spend more than I should.
— Anita Q., librarian

We've been fortunate to earn a good income, so much so that it's been years since we bothered to follow a budget. When it came time to file our income tax, I was shocked to realize we were in a higher tax bracket than expected. We had essentially been living beyond our means without realizing it. Making necessary changes, including reducing debt, will take a few years, but I'm already sleeping better at night.
— Alex T., salesperson

The Budgeting Process
Since setting a monthly budget is something of a lost art, here is an example of the process:

1. *Determine a realistic figure of your monthly expenses.* Estimate it if you haven't yet retired. Remember to include discretionary expenses for entertainment, vacation, membership fees, and gifts. Also remember to

calculate and include the monthly cost of things you pay for quarterly, bi-annually, and annually (e.g., property taxes, insurance, car registration, etc.).

2. *Calculate your monthly income.* This will include pension payouts, annuities, Social Security or Canada/ Quebec Pension Plan, income from bonds and/or preferred stock, and any employment income. Work with your financial advisor or accountant to determine the recommended distribution amount from IRAs or RRSPs.

3. *Account for regular contributions to savings for expected and unexpected expenses.* Expected expenses include the mundane, such as replacing your car, roof, furnace, appliances, etc. Expected expenses are also linked to any plans you make such as taking a special trip, remodelling your home, or helping someone pay for college. They might also include paying for help around the house as you get older, as well as funeral, cremation, or burial arrangements (if not taken care of already).

   As for saving for the unexpected, be realistic about what could happen, such as an injury from a fall or car accident, sudden illness, increased medication costs, temporarily supporting a family member, increased property taxes, or higher heating costs, as neither pulling the covers over your head nor imagining the sky will fall is going to help.

4. *Compare income to expenses.* If you're using estimates, use a conservative approach: the lower range for income and the higher range for expenses.

If your expenses are too high, create and implement a plan to reduce them, including reducing major expenses such as housing and/or expensive discretionary expenses such as a boat or a vacation home. Also evaluate whether working at a money job might be advisable or required.

If you need more help creating a monthly budget, talk to your financial advisor or banker. They would be pleased to assist you or at least refer you to someone who can. You can also go online and google "creating a personal budget."

Recommendations for Couples
If you're part of a couple and only one person has been managing the finances, it's time to change that system. Couples should calculate and manage budgets together. The more you communicate and work together now, the less likely you are to have costly surprises later on!

Once you have established your monthly budget, set time aside each month for you and your partner to update the information and prepare for the following month. If you or your partner is a little rusty on how to balance a chequebook or isn't familiar with online banking, add these topics into your "money talks."

It's amazing how time spent talking about budgeting enhances communication between partners and adds to their overall understanding and appreciation of money. On the other hand, money is one of the top three topics of arguments. If you're clashing on the topic, get help to work things out. Don't give up on managing finances together.

You're Old—Work it!

As part of your budget-smart thinking, remember to ask about senior discounts when attending concerts or movies, going to restaurants or museums, getting haircuts or pedicures, buying airline or train tickets, etc. Be sure to ask about such discounts even if the information isn't posted. Also be sure to ask small businesses such as dry cleaners and hair salons. Even if they don't have an official policy, they might offer you a discount anyway. You will be amazed how many organizations offer from 5 percent to 50 percent off the regular price in appreciation of their senior customers.

Chapter 12

Organize Papers and Research Services Before Needing Them— Success Strategy 5

This particular strategy encompasses two related areas:

1. Organizing your important papers and creating a reference document for others to use.
2. Educating yourself about services you or people close to you might someday need.

Organizing Your Papers and Creating a Reference Document

Far too many people have told me they didn't know where to find their loved one's important papers after they had passed away. This adds another layer of challenges to an already difficult time. Successful retirees take steps to prevent laying such a burden on their loved ones.

> *There is a saying: "Death is hardest to those it leaves behind." I don't intend to make it harder on my wife or children by leaving them a bunch of red tape to wade through.*
> —Joe D., office manager

When I say organize "papers," I'm not necessarily

referring to the need to create a will, trust, or powers of attorney. Rather, it's about something more prosaic and potentially more important: how to *find* the will, trust document, etc., as well how to find the papers associated with day-to-day living such as bank information, insurance information, and bills.

In addition to having problems locating the information described above, many people have also told me they had trouble determining who should be invited to the funeral and how to contact them. These people often express both guilt and anger for being placed in that situation.

Similar issues associated with papers and records occur when someone suffers a sudden debilitating injury or illness. In such cases, it's not a matter of "I've passed away, so it's not my problem." A lack of preparation will almost certainly affect you too.

Create a list of instructions and essential information to prevent these situations from occurring. Review it with your partner and/or children—anyone who might need to use it or help your loved ones with it. Also be sure they know where to find an updated list if you end up creating one.

Our father had suffered a serious stroke and was unable to communicate. Our mother was beside herself. After leaving the hospital, we kids decided to dig through their home office. Tucked into a file was a list of bank accounts, online banking and email passwords, contacts for his retirement fund, etc. We used that to help our mother keep the household running. Thanks to that file, we could

also contact his friends in town, who pitched in to ready the home for him—because he did eventually recover enough to come home.
—Don M., student

Below, you'll find examples of what you might want to cover in your list. I also recommend consulting with a financial advisor and perhaps an attorney to arrange a will, financial and health care powers of attorney, and trust if appropriate.

There are different types of powers of attorney (POA). Many only apply if you have passed away or are physically and/or mentally unable to handle your own affairs. The latter usually requires a confirmation of incompetency from two doctors, which is something many doctors are reluctant to give in today's litigious society. In addition, many financial organizations—banks, credit unions, investment firms, etc.—will not accept any POA that does not use their particular form.

Explore these issues in advance, including with each financial organization you use, and be sure to take the appropriate steps, including completing the appropriate forms with each organization before a POA is needed.

Information to Include in Your Reference Document

1. *People to be notified at the time of your death.* Certain people and institutions need to be notified of your death, including your lawyer, executor, trustee, and accountant, along with Canada/Quebec Pension Plan or Social Security authorities. Relatives and special friends will want to know as soon as possible, so providing the

names, addresses, and telephone numbers will make this task easier for your loved ones.

2. *Mortuary, cremation, and funeral arrangements.* Be sure to communicate any prepaid arrangements as well as your wishes (e.g., body burial, type of casket, cremation, hymn and music requests).

3. *The location of personal papers.* Give the exact location of important documents such as birth and marriage certificates, diplomas, military papers, etc. It's a good idea to gather these documents and store them in a single location such as a safety deposit box. Include certificates of insurance, deeds, and current mortgage papers. Also indicate where old mortgage documents are stored in case they are needed to resolve issues involved in property sale, etc.

4. *Bank accounts and bank locations.* List all bank accounts by name of institution, branch (if applicable), and type of account. Also provide the location of your safety deposit box and the location of the key. Be sure you specify the address, not just the name of the institution.

    If you're not married, or if you have beneficiaries in addition to or instead of your partner on certain accounts, list the beneficiaries and their contact information for each account.

    You might also wish to include a list of monthly household expenses. This makes it easier for someone to continue to pay bills if you are unable to. It also helps people recognize suspicious activity on the accounts. (A copy of your budget might suffice because monthly bills should be listed as part of it.)

5. *Passwords for online banking, phone accounts, email, and any other services*. Experts tell us not to write these down, but your loved ones might need to know how to access these accounts. You can disguise passwords in ways that only your loved ones could figure out (e.g., "The name of Suzie's first cat plus the number 168"). Just be sure to use references they will indeed know!

You can also create a reference document without account numbers and give it to someone you trust who is easily accessible, such as an adult child, a sibling, or a friend.

6. *Credit card and other loan accounts such as lines of credit*. List the issuer, card/account number, and customer service phone number. If you normally carry some but not all of your credit cards with you, provide that information so people will know if a card is missing from your wallet or purse.

7. *Insurance policies and survivor benefits*. List all life, auto, home, veterans, medical, and other insurance policies. List the agents' contact information or the customer service numbers and give the location of policy documents. As noted above for bank accounts, also list beneficiary information. Describe any loans you have taken out against any of your policies.

List all possible sources of benefits not already included in the above group (e.g., government pension, veterans pension, employee pension, fraternal associations, etc.).

Indicate sources of any income that roll over to your partner, and include information about amounts as well (e.g., the percentage of a pension that continues to be paid).

8. *Vehicles*. Indicate where the registration and other papers can be found for all vehicles you own, including cars, boats, ATVs, recreational vehicles, etc. Provide the location of all keys and any special operating instructions (e.g., "Jiggle the key to turn the ignition").

9. *Past income, property, and business tax information*. Provide the location of your personal and business income tax returns for the past three years. Do the same for property and business taxes, and be sure to note the due dates on the list of household bills. Provide your tax advisor's contact information and any special instructions.

10. *Investments, including mutual funds, stocks, and bonds*. List the location of your investment statements. List the names and contact information of all your financial advisors. If you own certificates of deposit, gold or silver coins, etc., provide the location(s) and pertinent details.

11. *The location(s) of valuables*. List all jewelry and other valuables such as special photographs, china, glass-

ware, art, etc., and their location(s). This list will also come in handy if you experience a theft. Your list can also include the names of people to whom the articles are to be given.

12. *Trusts, loans, and money owed to you.* List any trusts you have established, noting the location of the trust documents. Provide the names and contact information of the trustees. List all loans and other accounts receivable (money owed to you). Give full information on the terms and payments, including any wishes to forgive debt. Be as descriptive as possible.

13. *Preferred local assisted living residences, short-term skilled nursing facilities, in-home care providers, and other resources.* When such services and resources are needed, there is often little time to "shop" for the best options. Completing the research in advance and noting your preferences or best options will be useful in the future.

With a current will and the above list of information, you will feel more at ease that your wishes and final plans will be fulfilled. Your partner will also feel much more at ease knowing your death or a serious injury or illness won't create unnecessary difficulties as a result of not knowing where to find your documents and property.

There are many "organizers" on the market that guide you through a list similar to the above, and they usually include a binder so you can keep everything in one place. Some of these might be a good buy, but remember that you will still have to do the work of collecting and noting information, and you can simply purchase a suitable binder yourself.

Research Project

"I know that I know nothing."
— The Socratic Paradox

"Knowledge is power."
— Sir Francis Bacon

I could introduce this research project with a story of someone who spent their retirement savings far more quickly than expected. I have certainly heard many such stories. They were told by people who saw it happen to someone special: a parent, a relative, or a dear friend. Having witnessed what could happen, these people now do their best to avoid a similar catastrophe.

Seeing a beloved older person run into extreme financial difficulty leaves a profound impression. However, the stress and grief over a loved one's situation are only part of what sinks in. Valuable lessons also come from the firsthand knowledge gained when trying to help. For example, when arranging in-home care for a parent, we learn how much such care costs and how to shop for it. When researching assisted living residences for an uncle, we learn how to find the options, what questions to ask, and what expenses to expect. And when a situation becomes dire for a loved one, we learn a great deal about government-provided assistance or lack thereof.

Many successful retirees report this kind of hands-on

experience, but they don't let such knowledge make them despondent. Instead, they apply what they know in very practical and positive ways, including:

- being fully informed on personal budgeting and financial planning, including participating in what-if calculations with their financial advisor (e.g., "What if I need in-home care?");
- making informed decisions about where to live, especially as they grow older and enter the "slow-go" years; and
- making smart choices for health care, long-term care, and other types of insurance.

Fortunately, our loved ones don't have to experience distress to learn these valuable lessons. There is ample information on the Internet, and we can educate ourselves quite effectively from the comfort of our own home. By performing the research outlined below, you will do just that.

Before you get started, I'd like to share two additional points:

1. The research outlined below should be an integral part of planning for a successful retirement. I encourage you to complete it now. Don't let thoughts of far-off decisions and distant needs persuade you to delay.

2. Needing in-home care, assisted living, or government assistance shouldn't be a cause for embarrassment, but many people regard it as such. Let's rid ourselves of

this stigma. Talk frankly with your family and include information from your reference document. Share what you learn with others and ask them to share with you. Sharing knowledge is empowering!

Things to Research

1. *Residential options*. Use the Internet (and telephone) to learn more about several assisted living residences in your area or areas to which you might consider re-locating.

   Educate yourself on the variety of services and arrangements, including options for transitioning from independent living to assisted living to skilled nursing care (nursing home). Gather cost information. Determine whether facilities in other areas or different provinces or states provide better value at lower cost.

   You might also find visiting some assisted living residences informative—and perhaps quite pleasant!

2. *Care in your home*. Contact several reputable providers of in-home caregivers and gather information about cost. Be sure to ask about the rates for caregivers qualified to handle medications or special needs such as monitoring blood pressure and the rates for caregivers who don't have such qualifications. Also ask about the kinds of housekeeping or meal preparation the caregivers will or won't generally do.

   You might also want to ask friends about any independent caregivers they know of. This will give you a sense of the cost of these providers. Be sure to discuss any issues your friends have encountered. Be aware that working with independent caregivers has its pros and cons. Some pros might include possible lower salary costs compared to caregivers associated with an agency, more one-on-one care, and finding someone from your neighbourhood. A couple of cons might include requiring time to advertise, interview, and check references; a lack of direct supervision; being uninsured; and an incompatibility between the caregiver and recipient.

3. *Assistive devices in the home.* Determine the availability and cost of assistive living products such as raised toilet seats, shower seats, walk-in bathtubs, grab bars, bed rails, stair lifts, walkers, portable oxygen machines, etc.

4. *Other assistance.* You might also want to research the availability and cost of non-health assistance such as grocery shopping and other errands, meal preparation or delivery, transportation to and from doctor and other appointments, light or full housecleaning, yard maintenance and snow removal, etc.

Does your phone service provider or regulatory agency offer special phones for those who are hard of hearing, need extra-large buttons, etc.? These are available on the open market but might cost less through other sources.

Research the Safety Net
Be sure to research the safety net of last resort because many people imagine being able to get a level of support

that's far beyond reality. Details will undoubtedly change, but that's not the point of this particular recommendation. Completing this research now might inspire you to ensure that you never need to apply what you learn in this case. You might also be able to assist others when they are in need.

- *Canadian citizens*: Familiarize yourself with medical coverage provided by Medicare, including provincial limitations in costs and services. Focus on "residential long-term care" for the elderly, and consider the following questions: What financial conditions define eligibility? What options, if any, are available for care in your home as well as in residence in an assisted living facility or a nursing home? What is the likelihood the options will change given possible provincial budgetary constraints?

- *U.S. citizens*: Educate yourself about the Medicare programs including being a member of a Medicare Advantage plan. Understand the costs, coverage, and eligibility given the circumstances. Focus on "residential long-term care" for the elderly in your community and state. What types of facilities are available, cost, wait times, etc.

  Also, exercise extreme caution before engaging the services of so-called "Medicare planners." These services often cost thousands. Those whose financial situation precludes using advisors should seek free programs, which are readily available.

Chapter 13
Work with Mentors—
Success Strategy 6

With many people retiring earlier, you may find yourself
retired for ten, fifteen, twenty, twenty-five, thirty, or more
years. That's a long time! When we started in life, gaining
experience and maturing, we had many mentors along the
way—parents, family members, teachers, friends,
coaches, business associates, supervisors, and managers.
Those of us who raised a family also had mentors to help
us (parents, grandparents, friends). They all showed us the
way, pointed out the pitfalls, and helped us navigate
through the obstacles. They also encouraged and praised
us, and helped guide our actions.

Retirement is no different; it's filled with adventure,
change, and the unknown. Facing this new phase of your
life, you can choose to jump into retirement with both feet,
without any planning or discussion, or you can enter retirement fully prepared and with appropriate support and
guidance. Clearly, I advocate the latter.

As part of your retirement preparation, I encourage
you to find and use one or more mentors to provide you
with the advice and emotional support you'll need to be a
successful retiree.

The biggest "aha" moment in your talk about suc-
cessful retirement was when you brought up the

idea of using a mentor. I've had several mentors throughout my career. I've also paid good money to golf pros and personal trainers. Getting somebody involved in my retirement made instant sense to me, and I know the perfect guy.

—John K., senior executive

You will be glad to know that several ladies from our group have met our educational and social needs and found mentors in one fell swoop. We created a successful retirement study and accountability group!

—Jan F., foundation coordinator

How to Find a Mentor

Here are some tips for finding a suitable mentor:

1. *Acknowledge that it's difficult to have a successful retirement without help.* One or more mentors can assist you in developing your retirement vision and plan. They can play the devil's advocate to help hone your thinking. They can also provide you with ideas and options designed to achieve your retirement goals.

2. *Ask yourself if there are one or two people in your immediate family or social circle who can serve as your mentor.* Consider a work colleague or friend, someone who already has created a successful retirement plan, or someone who is already a retiree you admire. Before seeking them out, ask yourself the following questions: "Why do I consider this person

a good potential mentor?" "What is it about them I respect?" and "Would I be appreciative of their assistance and guidance?"

Be sure to consider your financial advisor as a potential mentor. Most are keenly interested in helping their clients achieve not only financial success but also total retirement success in all the aspects outlined in this book. In addition, many advisors are in the retirement business and as such have insights and experience that might be of use to you as you transition into life after work. At the very least, share your holistic vision and strategy of retirement with your financial advisor. Leave the door open for them to help you fine-tune your plan.

3. *Once you identify one or more potential mentors, meet with them individually.* Discuss the potential of establishing and maintaining a mentoring relationship, including the expectations and concerns, both yours and theirs. Also be sure to discuss the time commitment. Will you meet once every month or two to discuss your overall retirement progress? Will you have weekly or biweekly critiques of your retirement plan and actions?

Prepare to Give Back

Selecting a mentor and working together shouldn't be a one-way street. The secret of a good mentor relationship is for both parties to work toward building an effective and satisfying relationship. Mentoring is similar to other important relationships in life: It must be nurtured to reach its full potential. Here are a few ways to help deepen your mentoring relationship on both sides of the table:

1. Develop an understanding of each other's background and issues.
2. Develop an environment of mutual admiration.
3. Treat each other as confidants.
4. Be open to your mentor's ideas and suggestions.
5. Help each other focus on resolvable problems.
6. Avoid forcing your preferences and judgments on each other.
7. Develop a relationship that is meaningful and valuable for both parties.

Mentoring relationships are not something to enter into lightly. To produce worthwhile results, both parties need to make a solid commitment of time and energy. With the proper mix of dedication and caution, mentoring can immensely enrich your retirement and your life.

If you're having trouble finding a mentor, many senior centres offer peer counselling or coaching. You might find the mentor you seek at such places, enjoy being a peer counsellor or coach yourself, or both! Many people also work as a "life coach." These are people who help others set and achieve personal goals. Using such services can help you succeed in retirement.

Chapter 14
Put Things in Writing —
Success Strategy 7

This particular strategy for success helps introduce Part II of this book. In Part II, I encourage you to write things down. This suggestion might seem simple, like a no-brainer, but there is more to the value of writing than first meets the eye.

We live in a fast-paced world with tremendous convenience, and we love to get things done quickly. We rush around, moving from one project to the next with little or no time to think about what we've done and how we did it. However, if we are to be successful in our retirement life, we need to take time to reflect on our actions to see what worked, to see what could have been done differently, and to plan for our next challenges. The simple act of writing is a way to slow down and do all of that.

Successful retirees all stress the importance of having some sort of written record, including documentation of your retirement plan, actions taken, thoughts, perspectives, and observations.

Writing can also be an effective way to manage stress and enhance personal growth. It's easy to do, and it allows you to express your dreams, purpose in life, memories, and feelings.

What to Write

Whether you write lists, use Part II of this book, or keep a journal—or all three of these things—I encourage you to write

- your retirement vision as it progresses;
- your retirement plan, including goals, milestones, and actions;
- what worked or is working, and what didn't work or isn't working;
- your successes and the challenges yet to come; and
- your reflections, ideas, thoughts, and feelings on how your retirement is unfolding.

Remember, too, the question I posed at the beginning of this book:

Will you create the best retirement you can,
or will you let your retirement years just happen to you?

Writing is certainly a way to manage the details of your successful retirement. It's a tool to create the best retirement you can. But more than that, writing is a way to document your journey into a new way of living.

I sincerely hope your journey will be thought-provoking and rewarding. I wish you the best in living your retirement dream and leave you with these words from Napoleon Hill, author of the popular personal development book *Think and Grow Rich*:

"Cherish your visions and your dreams, as they are the

children of your soul, the blueprints of your ultimate achievements."

Part II

Creating Goals and Action Items

Chapter 15

The Power of Goals and Action Items

As described in Chapter 14, the process and results associated with writing deliver many benefits. Writing helps us slow down, focus, reflect, think, and organize our thoughts. Writing is also an effective way to manage stress, a way to vent and achieve.

The process of writing is a fundamental building block for creating a plan for a successful retirement. The results help document our plan and give us extremely important tools for implementing the plan.

Part II of the book, Creating Goals and Action Items, allows you to unlock the power of writing. It's designed to help you create and implement your own unique retirement vision and plan. In short, it will help make your idea of a successful retirement a thriving reality.

Before you get started, I recommend you read through this chapter carefully, as it introduces you to Part II and includes information on how to use goals and action items, general tips for using Part II, and frequently asked questions. You might also want to scan through the rest of Part II before getting started to familiarize yourself with its approach, layout, and contents. As you do, please note the following:

1. Much of the content here in Part II is directly related to the content in Part I. (The relevant chapter headings indicate this.)

2. The content and layout differ from section to section (chapter to chapter) because the nature of the tasks and/or issues differs.

How to Use Goals and Action Items

Almost any type of planning and implementation process involves completing certain actions to reach goals. Part II walks you through that process, chapter by chapter, element by element, using goals and action items. Goals and action items are often shown in a set on a single page. (See the following example.)

Goals

Goals come first so you know what you're working toward. You'll see recommended goals as well as one or two blank lines so that you can add your own goals as desired.

Note the column titled "By." Use this column if you wish to set deadlines or target dates. Setting and meeting deadlines is a great motivator!

Also note the boxes to the left of each goal. These are provided so you can check off each goal as you achieve it.

For couples: Although some goals are designed specifically for couples, most are written as for an individual. Discuss this as a couple and decide whether you will each meet a given goal or share the goal.

Action Items

Action items are essentially things on a to-do list—the things you need to do to reach each goal. There are no complete lists of action items because these to-dos are unique for each person or couple. Instead, you'll see one or two examples along with plenty of space to write down your own action items.

Which Comes First, Goals or Action Items?

Goals are shown above action items to guide your efforts and focus. However, you might have to take certain actions to inform your goals, and so you'll often work on completing action items first.

Goals and Action Items (Example)

(For the entertainment element of a balanced leisure lifestyle)

Goals: **By**

☐ Schedule activities in my calendar so   _____
   I'm regularly reminded to follow
   through (e.g., monthly).

☐ Set and follow an entertainment budget.   _____

☐ Couples: We have selected and   _____
   scheduled regular shared activities.

☐ _____

   (A blank line is provided so you can add a goal if desired.)

Action Items: **By**

Start a newspaper subscription so I get
the entertainment section. Check into
memberships and/or discounts at the
zoo and museums.   May 24

_____   _____

_____   _____

_____   _____

_____   _____

Check off goals as you reach them and cross out action items when completed. These small acts have a big impact because they help you recognize and feel the progress you're making.

General Tips for Using Part II

1. Part II is organized using the same chapters and flow as Part I. Review the relevant chapter to refresh yourself on the objectives, recommendations, issues, and guidelines. Such review will also help you focus and work more productively.

2. Use the pages of this book to capture your vision and your plans of action. List action items in the area provided, setting deadlines as needed. Be sure to include things you plan to discuss with your partner and mentor(s).

3. Use this part of the book to track your progress as well. The primary goals are shown. Check them off as you reach them. When you have completed an action item, cross it off the list. Be sure to check and cross off by hand even if you're typing out your plan and action items. It's a *wonderful* feeling to physically draw a line through an achieved action item!

4. You might wish to avoid using this workbook section for drafting ideas and taking miscellaneous notes because that can clutter the pages, making them difficult to use as a reference and guide. Consider using a separate blank notebook for things such as

    *   notes from brainstorming sessions;
    *   drafts of lists;
    *   ideas, questions, concerns;
    *   possible resources; and

- names of people who might help you.

5. Many people also like to keep a journal, a place where they write their thoughts and feelings, and perhaps sketch. This could be part of the above-mentioned notebook or kept separate to maintain privacy.

6. Please note that typing your action item lists, brainstorm notes, questions, journal, etc., is just as effective as handwriting. Do what is most convenient and comfortable for you.

Frequently Asked Questions

1. Should I go through each chapter in order?

The first chapter of Part II repeats an exercise from Part I: Your Current Picture. If you haven't already completed this exercise, I recommend doing so before doing anything else. Other than that, the order of completion is up to you. However, keep in mind that some chapters/activities inform or otherwise affect others. For example, completing a budget could affect your planning for where you want to live, or visa versa. Also, finding a mentor early will help you create—and implement—your overall plan.

Also keep in mind that nurturing your creative side is an aspect of a successful retirement. Feeling a need to do something in a particular order sometimes inhibits creativity. Some people choose to tackle the "hard" parts first, while others do the "easy" parts first. If you're prone to procrastination, the former is recommended.

2. I'm a big believer in setting deadlines. Shouldn't each and every action item and goal have a deadline?

I too am a big believer in setting and meeting deadlines. I'm also a big believer in everyone taking ownership of their own successful retirement. In addition, many aspects of a successful retirement are continual. For example, including entertainment in your life isn't something you do once and it's done for good. Here are a few ideas for managing deadlines:

- Use the "By" space to set and keep deadlines as it makes sense, and if it helps motivate you to complete tasks. Setting deadlines is especially useful if you're prone to procrastination. Also consider asking someone to hold you accountable for meeting your deadlines.

- Bring big tasks and their associated deadlines down to a manageable size by using milestones—markers along the way. For example, if you've set a goal of moving to a new home by the end of next year, milestones might include: sorting through possessions by March, asking friends for referrals to realtors by April, researching new areas by August, etc.

- Setting a specific period for a new activity can help set good habits. This isn't a deadline, per se, but you can certainly use the "By" space for it:

Action Items: **By**

Buy more fresh fruits or vegetables
each time I shop.   3 *months*

3. My partner and I are excited about planning for the next phase of our life together. Should we do all of this as a couple?

That's wonderful! In healthy relationships, each partner has their own interests and activities in addition to shared interests and activities. A healthy approach to planning and implementation should reflect that. Although what's best will differ from couple to couple, here are some things to consider:

- Most people find it easier to reflect and visualize on their own. Do this and then come together to discuss things and make joint decisions.

- In many relationships, one person has stronger opinions about certain things. (In some relationships, one person has stronger opinions about everything.) If this is true for you and your partner, the person with a stronger opinion should take a step back and encourage the other person to fully express themselves first. Remember to practice active listening along with other communication skills (see Chapter 10: Improve Communication).

- Some couples have shared with me that they knew in advance which topics they were likely to disagree on. This expectation can actually help if it means you'll approach the topic with greater sensitivity. Unfortunately, advance awareness of touchy topics can also have negative effects. Review Chapter 10 for tips on how to avoid this.

- In many relationships, one person does more of certain tasks than the other person. Typical examples include paying the bills, washing the dishes, and taking out the garbage and recycling. One half of a couple might also be considered better at something. For example, maybe one of you is better at math. Don't let familiar roles completely drive who does what in visualizing, planning, and implementation. This is an excellent time to more equally distribute work if you wish. You might even enhance your relationship by expanding your understanding of each other's abilities.

- On the other hand, it often makes sense to divide tasks between you. For example, you might agree to each research six options for entertainment. That gives you a total of twelve to consider together! One of you might be better at using the Internet to research new areas to live, but you'll explore them together and in person.

4. I went to your program by myself because my partner was not interested. Should I try to make him participate in the planning?

This question/concern comes up often. "Should I make my partner create a plan?" "Should I nag, beg, bribe…?" Similar questions and concerns come up about one person doing more work than the other. There is no single answer because there are so many versions of successful relationships. However, here are some tips for handling things when your partner doesn't want to participate:

- Don't nag or beg. Focus on your own visualizing and planning in a positive way. Your activities can lead by example, as well as accomplish a lot for the both of you.

- Some couples "bribe" or negotiate to make agreements, as in: "If you do this, I will do that." If this has worked well for you in the past, it will probably work well in planning and implementing a successful retirement.

- As you visualize and plan, share your thoughts with your partner and specifically ask for their input and suggestions. For example:

  "What have I missed?"
  "Tell me about changes you would suggest."
  "Anything jump out at you that could pose a problem?"
  "I'm stuck on something. Will you help me?"

- Use active listening as your partner answers, and thank your partner for any ideas, thoughts, or direction offered. Be prepared for most of these comments to be critical because most of us find it easier to criticize. Many men, especially, tend to problem-solve by looking most at what needs to be "fixed." You can take some of the sting out of this by purposefully asking for negative feedback first. Doing so helps you mentally prepare for it. One of the best ways to get positive feedback is to ask for it: "Talk to me about what you think are the strengths in this plan so far." Regularly asking for positive feedback might even "train" your partner to give it without being asked.

- If a discussion becomes a fight, let it go for a while. Give yourself and your partner a chance to think and cool down. Conversely, if you felt pushed or talked into something but didn't speak up at the time, don't let it be; speak up as soon as possible.

- Push on the most important issues. In other words,

pick your battles. Working together on where to live is probably more important than ensuring both of you have educational pursuits.

- Be careful of armchair psychological analysis. Playing therapist can create more obstacles and pushback. It might look to you that your partner is in denial, afraid of getting old, etc., and it might indeed be the case, but it's just as likely your partner is processing in their own way and on their own schedule.

- Get help if needed, including counseling from spiritual leaders, trusted friends, or counsellors.

5. When I think of retirement and retirement planning, I'm excited, but I'm also afraid. To be honest, there are times I feel quite overwhelmed. Is this normal?

This is absolutely normal! The prospect of change and facing the unknown often generates feelings of fear and anxiety. As humans, we all have fears of one sort or another. On the positive side, fear helps us protect ourselves and those we love. For example, the fear of being in a traffic accident prompts us to use seatbelts and to ensure others in the car do too. On the negative side, fear can ensnare our motivation to take action and stop us from trying something new. Fear can even escalate to the point of overtaking our rational thinking. Here are some actions you can take to help yourself overcome fears—big and small—about retirement:

- Actively practice positive thinking. Keep reminding

yourself how fortunate you are to have things such as a loving family, dear friends, reasonably good health, and a life in a free country—make a point to identify positive things in your life.

- Acknowledge your strengths and ability to adapt. Think about changes you have already managed successfully, including adolescence, completing an education, buying a home, raising a family, and navigating a career.

- Share your fears with people you love and respect. They can provide needed support, perspective, and ideas. They can also nudge you out of self-created ruts.

- Collaborate on important issues. For instance, if you fear running out of money, talk to your financial advisor to see if the fear is valid. If need be, work together to restructure your financial portfolio to improve the situation.

- If the entire prospect of retirement or planning is overwhelming, use this part of the book to break things into smaller steps or goals. If a certain issue, step, or goal generates a sense of trepidation, break it into smaller steps too. Either way, the key is to focus on each one in turn, not the big picture.

- Make finding a mentor a priority. Find someone who can guide and support you.

- Get professional help such as counselling or psychotherapy if fear prevents you from making progress with your retirement plans.

6. Our children have strong opinions about where we should live, whether we should sell or rent our home, etc. We appreciate their concern, but they're driving us crazy. How should we handle this?

I encourage you to begin by openly discussing the hopes and concerns that lie behind your children's opinions. Do they hope to have you live nearer so they can spend more time with you or have you care for the grandkids? Are they worried you will run out of money or be unsafe in your home? These discussions might cover topics you would prefer to keep private, and the choice whether to reveal the information is extremely personal. You might, however, find that sharing information about your thorough planning, including your use of this book, will be enough to assuage their concerns.

Listen to your children's ideas and feedback because they will add other perspectives to your retirement planning, but you need to balance that with maintaining your independence in handling your own affairs and decisions.

7. Should we announce our intention to retire in advance?

There's no single answer to this question. Let's look at some of the career issues first. Self-employed individuals, people in key company positions, and people who work closely with customers and prospects should consider whether the announcement would prompt the loss of business. It might be best to ensure that continuity and support are clearly in place before making the announcement.

People lower on the organizational ladder might also experience unexpected consequences. Supervisors and colleagues might see your retirement planning as "bailing out" and make your work life miserable in the meantime. You might also miss out on being offered a retirement package, as employers don't need to offer an incentive to those who have already decided to retire.

As for letting friends and family know, although they are usually concerned for our welfare and appreciate being part of our planning, you should again consider potential career issues. If friends and family — and their friends and family — work in the same circles as you, the news might come out before you wish it to. This is now much more possible than in the past thanks to social networks such as Facebook.

8. I have heard certain times of the year are better for taking the step into retirement. Is this true?

Yes, there are some timing issues to consider. Let's start with financial matters:

- If your employer has a pension plan, RRSP or 401K plan, or other retirement program, be sure to find out how certain retirement dates affect the specific benefit amount as well as the timing of any cost-of-living in-creases. Be sure to factor vesting schedules into the timing equation.

- Evaluate how vacation days, sick time, or other paid

time off (PTO) accrue, carry over, and are paid out upon retirement. Also consider the payment of bonuses, commissions, and any draws if those apply. Investigate how timing will affect any stock options as well.

- Investigate how timing will affect health care plan options as well as premiums. Seek help from the human resources department to find needed information and discuss options. Consider attending the retirement workshops many employers offer as well.

  It might also be important to discuss some or all of the above with a qualified financial planner or CPA. Whether you're employed or self-employed, consult with a tax professional well before choosing a time to retire (at least one to two years prior). Revisit the issues regularly to help determine more exact timing.

  In addition to the above, consider what's going on with the company itself. How might the company stock price or other financial factors affect things, for better or worse? What's the probability of being offered a "package" or other incentive to retire? Again, consult with appropriate professionals to evaluate these issues as they apply.

Retiring at a certain time of year has pros and cons to consider as well:

- November and December might be ideal, as this is a time of completion, celebration, and planning for the New Year. You might also be better able to enjoy the holidays with loved ones. On the other hand, you might miss attending work-oriented holiday events or feel out of place if you do attend.

- Retiring at a certain time of year has pros and cons in terms of the weather too. Pay particular attention to the effect the weather might have on the inaugural weeks of your retirement. January through March usually includes many gray, cold days further north, which will add a bleak feeling early on in your retirement. On the other hand, the months of "June gloom" can feel quite oppressive in some areas further south.

    Whatever season you choose, ensure to proactively plan activities and follow through. Take a trip to warmer or cooler climes, plan several ski trips in the winter, sign up for a gardening club to fully enjoy spring, volunteer to take the grandkids to swim class to make the most of summer—whatever helps you enjoy those first months of retirement.

9. Once I've completed my plan and am living a holistic and well-balanced retirement, how often should I re-evaluate or redo the plan?

Although it might not be necessary to redo your entire plan, it's important to regularly revisit your plan and make adjustments. By remaining proactive and using a "living" retirement plan, you will be sure to get the best of the second longest phase of your life. I recommend re-evaluating your plan and gauging progress at least once a year, including comparing how actual activities match up against your planned activities.

In addition, there are certain situations that call for re-evaluating and adjusting your plan. Here is an overview of the most common situations with some tips on how to deal with them:

- *You half-heartedly completed parts of the plan or skipped some things entirely.* Let's face it: We're only human! Don't waste time beating yourself up; take action. Reread Part I, use Part II to plan, and then follow through.

- *You or your partner often feel unhappy or feel that something "isn't right."* Although it's advisable to review your entire plan, I suggest you start by taking a close look at the elements of living a balanced leisure lifestyle. You might find adjustments in that area quickly make a positive impact. (See Chapters 3 and 17.)

  If you and your partner created the plan together, it might help if each of you evaluates the plan and status of your retirement on your own. Consider whether you participated in planning and implementation as much as you should have, or perhaps too much. Think about the times you "gave in" or pushed your significant other to do that. After you both have had time for reflection, come together to discuss, revise, and implement changes to the plan.

- *A major change has occurred.* Major changes can be negative or positive! The most common negative changes include losing a partner through death or divorce, and experiencing a decline in health. Financial difficulty, including a significant decline in the value of assets, is also common. Less common negative changes include natural disasters such as fire, earthquake, or flood. Revamping your plan and implementing changes will help make the most of the new situation.

Among the most common examples of positive changes include marrying or cohabitating with a significant other. Home values might increase enough for you to consider selling and moving elsewhere. A child or grandchild might move in (you choose whether that would be positive or negative). Other positive changes include winning the lottery or inheriting a substantial sum of money. These positive changes are reasons to re-evaluate your plan too.

Chapter 16

Two Exercises to Get You Started

Exercise 1: Visualizing Your Current Picture of Retirement

Early in this book, I recommended beginning your planning for a successful retirement by visualizing what "retirement" currently means to you. If you haven't already done so, I urge you to visualize that now before tackling other parts of the plan. Below, you will find the worksheet "Visualizing Your Current Picture of Retirement," where you can list your goals and action items for this exercise.

Whether you're preparing to retire or are already retired, you probably have thoughts, feelings, and images connected to the concept of retirement. Some are likely positive, and some negative; some are likely realistic, and some not.

Negative and unrealistic thoughts and images will undermine your ability to enjoy success. One purpose of this exercise is to uncover these so you can deal with them. Positive and realistic thoughts and images are strengths to build upon. Another purpose of this exercise is to uncover these so you can construct your plan more easily.

Tips for Completing This Exercise
Here are some tips for picturing your current retirement, including ways to spark visualization:

- *Find a quiet place to reflect, take walks, go for long drives, and talk things over with friends or your partner.* These are all things that can help bring your current picture to the surface. They will present several opportunities for you to reveal your thoughts, ideas, images, etc. You might find varying the methods helps too. For example, take walks on some days but sit and reflect on other days.

- *Don't expect or strive for a cohesive or coherent picture.* Few people actually think or visualize that way! The important thing is to allow your thoughts, ideas, and images to flow so you have opportunities to work with them.

- *Write things down.* This helps many people process things more effectively, but having a written resource also makes it easier to apply certain elements as planning develops.

- *If it's not clear in the moment, there's no need to decide whether things are positive or negative.* In fact, forcing that judgment can be counterproductive. Simply note these thoughts and circle back for more consideration. As you later consider your thoughts, you might find that there is still no clear positive or negative. That's fine! Try adding "neutral" to the mix and see if that helps the process.

- *Don't try to over-organize your thoughts at this time.* Rather, use the fruits of this exercise as you complete the rest of Part II. Increased organization will occur as you proceed through the exercises.

Two elements of holistic retirement planning are often particularly helpful for visualization:

1. Picture yourself waking up.... What happens next? How do you spend your time?

2. Picture your surroundings.... Let your mind's eye include your current home, an imagined home, a current or imagined vacation home, visiting familiar and unfamiliar places or people. Where do you spend your time?

Here are some questions that can also help you get started:

- Do you look forward to going to bed and getting up whenever you want?
- Do you want to spend more time with your children, grandchildren, or partner? How about friends?
- Do people in your life have certain expectations of you once you retire? How do you feel about that?
- Does retirement mean you're getting "old"?
- Does retirement mean leaving work you love and/or co-workers you consider friends?
- Do you look forward to having more time to take care of yourself? Are you concerned about what might happen to your health?
- What does "retirement" mean for doing things you've wanted to do for years? Are you worried about not

having enough things to do, of being bored?

- Does your partner express concern or joke about you "being in their way"?
- Do you see this as a time to more fully enjoy, or rekindle, your relationship with your significant other? Or is this a time with more ominous portents?

Visualizing Your Current Picture of Retirement

Goals:	By
☐ My current picture of retirement is captured in a way that makes it easy to use in my future planning. (Writing it down is recommended.)	_____ _____ _____ _____ _____
☐ Couples: We have decided whether to share and/or discuss our current pictures. If so, we have followed through.	_____ _____ _____ _____
☐ _____	_____
☐ _____	_____
☐ _____	_____

Action Items:	By
Clear an entire weekend and then spend it on pondering, etc.	*Aug 17*
_____	_____
_____	_____
_____	_____
_____	_____
_____	_____
_____	_____
_____	_____
_____	_____
_____	_____

Exercise 2: Identifying Your New Roles

What we do for a living often defines how we see ourselves. What you do changes in retirement, and it's time to redefine your roles. Although your new roles might change over time, this exercise is designed to help you make that first transition more quickly and comfortably.

Tips for Completing This Exercise

Picture yourself chatting with someone in a setting such as a party or in line at the coffee shop. Someone asks, "What do you do?" What's the first response that comes to mind?

- *Is the response "Nothing"?* Even if you smile as you imagine saying it, "nothing" won't satisfy you for long. Work through building a balanced leisure lifestyle (see Chapters 3 and 17), paying close attention to education, hobbies, and social activities (and perhaps travel). Find something to replace that "nothing."

- *Does the response focus on your past work?* Try several versions of this sentence until it feels right: "I used to [your former profession or work], and now I...." Be sure to practice inserting a *positive* statement. Be sure to use the word *and* instead of *but*.

- *Do you have trouble coming up with a statement of what you do now?* Building a balanced leisure lifestyle will help. (See Chapters 3 and 17.) In the meantime, experiment with some versions of the following statements: "I'm freshly retired and experimenting with many new endeavours. How about you?" and "I was [your former profession or work], and I'm now retired and enjoying [an activity you already enjoy]. And you?" Be sure to prepare yourself to respond to follow-up questions about any new endeavours you're considering or planning for. Also notice how the statements end with a question about the other person. This tried-and-true networking technique will help expand your social circle!

Identifying Your New Roles

Goals: By
☐ I have completed this exercise.   _____
☐ _____   _____

You might find that there are no action items to set. The space below is provided as an option.

Action Items: By

_____   _____
_____   _____
_____   _____
_____   _____
_____   _____
_____   _____
_____   _____
_____   _____
_____   _____
_____   _____

Tips for Using These Exercises in the Future
Both of these exercises will provide value throughout your years of retirement.

- *Exercise 1: Visualizing Your Current Picture of Retirement*

    Revisit this exercise as a way to test or check in on your progress. How does your current picture match up with your vision? If you and your partner are in conflict, repeating this exercise might help clarify your respective wants and needs as well as enhance your ability to communicate.

- *Exercise 2: Identifying Your New Roles*

    Our roles can change many times throughout our retirement years. Revisit this exercise whenever—if ever—you're feeling down about yourself or unsure of your role(s). Working through Chapter 3 again might help identify how your role(s) have changed.

Chapter 17

Applying Chapter 3 (The Need for a Balanced Leisure Lifestyle)

This chapter covers six different areas because a balanced leisure lifestyle includes activity in six areas. The approach to helping you achieve balance is simple: Each element includes examples along with goals and action items.

The Overall Goal: Create and Maintain a Balanced Leisure Lifestyle

Your overall goal is to have *at least one regular activity in each area*. Here is a checklist to help you reach this goal the first time:

☐ Entertainment: Things you do for fun

☐ Education: Things you do to stretch your thinking, skills, and abilities

☐ Travel: Whether it's to far-off lands or the next province or state

☐ Exercise: Regular physical activity

☐ Social activities: Things you do with family, friends, and acquaintances

☐ Hobbies: Making things or developing a special expertise

Tips for Creating a Balanced Leisure Lifestyle

Below are tips to help you begin planning your balanced leisure lifestyle:

- *Make copies of the blank goals and action items pages before you begin.* Creating balance is not something you do once and you're done for good. Reuse the pages of examples, goals, and action items many times. The things you do to achieve and enjoy a balanced leisure lifestyle will change over time as your interests and situation change. Having blank copies of this part of the book will come in handy.

- *Don't worry about completing this chapter in the order it's presented.* Jump right into the element that most interests you, or consider tackling the one that's currently the weakest. Do whatever inspires you to get started on this part of planning a successful retirement.

- *Be careful about how you use deadlines.* A balanced and thriving leisure lifestyle isn't static. Don't let meeting initial goals or completing action items lull you into letting things slide.

- *Strive for true balance.* There are many activities that fulfill two or more areas at once. For example, joining a book club can be both social and educational, and working with Habitat for Humanity or participating in similar projects in other places is a hobby that often involves travel. On the other hand, some activities fulfill two or more areas on paper, but pushing it too far might undermine having a truly balanced lifestyle. For example, building sets for the community theatre might be a great social activity and hobby, but it shouldn't count as entertainment just because it takes place near a stage.

Entertainment

- **Theatre, shows, comedy clubs**
- **Concerts and recitals**
- **Sporting events**
- **Museums, aquariums, etc.**
- **Festivals, fairs, parades**
- **Movies**
- **Parties**
- **Tours, parks**
- **Regular date night**

Goals: **By**

☐ Set and follow _____ entertainment
   budget (e.g., monthly).   _____

☐ Schedule activities in my/our calendar
   for the next three months on a rolling
   basis.   _____

☐ Couples: Discuss and schedule shared
   vs. individual activities.   _____

☐ _____   _____

Action Items: **By**

*Start a subscription to the paper so
I get the entertainment section. Check
into memberships or discounts at the
Metropolitan Museum of Art.*   *May 24*

_____   _____

_____   _____

_____   _____

_____   _____

_____   _____

_____   _____

Education

- Classes of all kinds
- Learn or relearn a craft
- Complete a degree
- Lectures
- Be a docent or tour guide
- Learn a new language
- Genealogy research
- Take online courses
- Special museum tours

Goals: By

☐ Choose at least one educational
  activity I'll regularly participate in
  for the next _____ months.   _____

☐ Set any needed budget (e.g., cost of
  entry, supplies, transportation).   _____

☐ Couples: Discuss and schedule
  shared vs. individual activities.   _____

Action Items: By

Get the University Club lecture schedule.
Choose some lectures we both want to
attend. Check out the memoir writing
class. Am I brave enough to try it?   Aug 1

_____   _____

_____   _____

_____   _____

_____   _____

_____   _____

_____   _____

Travel

People are often tempted to leave this element out of their life. Don't do it! Whether your travels are big or small—no matter how you would define those—have some travel in your life. To enjoy the benefits of travel, I suggest taking these three steps below:

Step 1
Choose at least one of these overarching goals for travel:

☐ I will plan and take _____ (number) major trips every _____ (time frame).e.g., "I will plan and take one major trip every three years."
☐ I will plan and take _____ (number) small trips every _____ (time frame).e.g., "I will plan and take one small trip every year."

Step 2
Brainstorm a list of possible trips and then choose from that list. Try not to second-guess or analyze these as you brainstorm. Let your thoughts flow.

☐ I have created a list of possible trips, including dream-big trips and day trips.
☐ I have identified my top two or three possible trips and selected _____ (number) trips to work with as a start.

Step 3

Complete goals and action items for each trip selected. A blank set is provided, but make copies so you have several to work with! Also be sure to review the tips and example goals and action items below.

☐ I have made copies of the blank goals/action items travel sheet.
☐ I have created goals and action items for each trip in my first set of trips.

Travel: Tips and Example Goals and Action Items

Remember that travel need not be worldly or expensive. However, if you haven't travelled very far up to this point, I encourage you to stretch toward new and more distant horizons!

Should the thought of travelling farther or to unfamiliar places prompt any anxiety, try working up to it. Plan trips a bit farther away or a tiny bit more adventurous than you have previously. Follow through and stretch a bit farther next time. Other than that, there are two key things that will help you enjoy this element of a balanced leisure lifestyle:

1. Set a deadline or target for each trip. Otherwise, it's far too easy to let things get in the way.

2. Determine the budget and implement a savings plan if needed.

Some travel involves a set budget (e.g., a particular cruise might have a set cost). Other travel involves more choice and flexibility, where you'll have to set a budget and work from there. Either way, budgeting is a great idea, as is creating a savings plan when needed.

Trip / Travel:

Go to East Coast to see the autumn leaves. Fall 20—

Goals:	By
☐ **Complete research.**	Mar 20—
☒ **Establish a set budget or range.**	
$1,500 to $2,000	Jun 20—
☒ **Savings plan has been set and implemented (if needed).**	Done
☐ Apply tax refund and save $75 a month.	

Action Items:	By
See if Road Scholar (Elderhostel) has a trip.	Dec 20—
Build up walking stamina on Mt. Seymour trails.	Start now
~~Ask cousin Alan if I can stay with them a few nights.~~ Yes.	ASAP
~~Buy or borrow a better camera.~~ Gift from daughters!	Feb 20—

The above is just a partial example of common action items. See the next page for a blank goals and action items sheet, and remember to make copies.

Trip / Travel:

Goals: **By**

☐ Complete research.   _____

☐ Establish a set budget or range.   _____

☐ Savings plan has been set and   _____
   implemented (if needed).   _____

☐ _____   _____

☐ _____   _____

Action Items: **By**

Ask Jim if he's interested in a
fishing trip. Michigan? Discuss trip
with just us or with inviting wives,
kids, and grandkids.   Thanksgiving

_____   _____

_____   _____

_____   _____

_____   _____

_____   _____

_____   _____

Exercise

- Join a health club
- Go dancing or take a class
- Exercise at home
- Classes at rec centres
- Daily walks
- Take grandkids to the park
- Golf (especially walking instead of riding carts)
- Swim, hike, bike, bowl, skate

Goals: By

☐ Discuss options and issues with
  my doctor.   _____

☐ Find at least one exercise I can and
  will do two to three times a week.   _____

☐ Set and apply budget (equipment, class
  or membership fee, etc.).   _____

Action Items: By

*Borrow Cecilia's Wii U to see if
I like " Wii Fit U." Put up notice
at dog park to find dog-walking
partner.*   *May 15*

_____   _____

_____   _____

_____   _____

_____   _____

_____   _____

_____   _____

Social Activities

Activities that enlarge your social circle and nurture good relationships

• Participating in plays or shows
• Service clubs (e.g., Optimists, Rotary)
• Interests clubs (e.g., book club, knitting club)
• Regular volunteering activities
• Regular paid work activities
• Planned regular get-togethers with friends

Goals: **By**

☐ Choose at least one social activity I
  will participate in at least every
  two weeks.   _____

☐ Add to calendar, scheduling ahead
  as much as possible.   _____

☐ Set and apply budget (e.g.,
  membership, supplies, meals, etc.).   _____

☐ _____   _____

Action Items: **By**

See if Community Playhouse needs
any help with set-building. Accept
Suzanne's offer to be her guest at
women's group.   Feb 1

_____   _____

_____   _____

_____   _____

Hobbies

- Numerous crafts
- Local restoration projects
- Research family history
- Foster cats or dogs
- Sew quilts for kids in hospital
- Join a community garden
- Birdwatching
- Reenactment groups
- Writing, photography

Goals: By

☐ Choose at least one hobby I
   will enjoy at least _____
   (e.g., every week).   _____

☐ Set and apply budget (e.g., cost of
   class, supplies, etc.).   _____

☐ _____   _____

Action Items: By

*Take the grandkids to the little train
in Tilden Regional Park before the
summer ends. Talk to the guys there
about joining the restoration effort.*   *Aug 25*

_____   _____

_____   _____

_____   _____

Chapter 18
Applying Chapter 4 (Working and Volunteering)

Working and volunteering can help you build and maintain a successful retirement. The added structure and the opportunities to meet new people and develop new skills are just a few of the benefits. It should also be noted that many successful retirees work at paid jobs out of necessity. Please don't let concerns over such work "looking bad" keep you from earning needed money.

Use this chapter as you consider working for pay or volunteering. You can also use it as a tool to help guide you through your experiences. Although working for pay is covered separately from volunteering, there are two shared issues:

1. Be mindful of the time commitments involved as you consider working at paid and/or volunteer jobs. Be sure to include the time you are likely to spend commuting as well as engaging in activities such as chatting after volunteer event meetings or after working hours.

2. Avoid thinking that the work or volunteer activity and environment will be enough to create a successful retirement. They won't. Even those who work or volunteer full-time report that their lives are significantly

different than they were before retirement. It's still vital to plan, implement, and maintain a balanced retired life. Indeed, as mentioned in Chapter 3, achieving such balance is desirable whether you're retired or not.

Looking for and Working at a Money Job

- *Consult with a professional before you begin your search.* Many retirees are not aware that RRSP or IRA distributions, pension payments, annuities, and CPP/QPP or Social Security payments are considered income. Adding income via a paycheque can affect your tax bracket. For U.S. citizens, it can also affect Social Security benefits and Medicare premiums. Consult with an appropriate advisor on these matters before you begin your job search. Consult yet again before accepting a job. Don't expect a potential or new employer to guide you, as even human resource professionals rarely have this expertise.

- *Consider including your former employers in the search.* Many employers are amenable to hiring senior former employees. Explore the possibility of full- or part-time work, including on a contract basis. If you haven't previously worked as an independent contractor, reach out to someone who is familiar with the issues for guidance and insight. This is in addition to consulting with an advisor as mentioned above.

- *Consider retail, food service, seasonal positions, and customer service.* Retail includes shops, whether department stores or supermarkets. Food service includes fast food and other restaurants. Seasonal work includes clerking during the holidays or working at resorts or parks during their winter or summer peak seasons. Seasonal work also includes working at special events such as fairs and festivals. Many employers like to hire seniors for customer service in call centres, as they tend to be calmer and have a broad perspective as customers themselves, which translates to providing excellent service.

- *Consider businesses associated with a particular expertise or hobby.* Retired electricians, carpenters, and plumbers can find themselves as valued employees at hardware stores or specialty stores. People who knit, crochet, sew, and make jewelry are in similar demand at stores providing related supplies and classes. These jobs often provide a high level of enjoyment and satisfaction in addition to the extra income.

- *Consider service companies who hire people with professional expertise.* Pharmacies, hospitals, and health care plan providers often provide advice services by telephone. Many organizations outsource accountants, executives, and others on a temporary or contract basis. Expertise in these and other areas make you ideal for such jobs.

- *Do some research and be willing to step outside of your comfort zone.* Options tend to depend on the area in which you live and the economy. Here are just a few of the jobs you might find available in addition to those already mentioned:

- Paid tutor.
- Courtesy shuttle driver.
- Office clerk or manager, bank teller.
- Fundraiser (over the phone).

- Substitute teacher (previous teaching experience may not be required).

When researching your options, you might need to search both online job boards and classified ads. Don't let lack of Internet savvy hold you back! In addition, speak with local business owners. Let them know you're looking, and ask about the kinds of jobs they might have open at some point. Be sure to stay in touch. Extend similar networking efforts to your friends and acquaintances as well.

Interviewing for a Money Job

- *If it's been quite a while since you interviewed for a job, prepare yourself.* Be ready to interview no matter how "menial" the job might be. Practice responses to the following questions:

  1. What work experience do you have that will apply in this job?
  2. Which of your personal attributes will you use and/or will provide value?

- *Be sure to ask the interviewer your own questions.* Some questions you can prepare in advance might include the following:

1. Questions that help you put your best foot forward. For example: "I'm told I'm very patient. How might this help me be a good service representative for your organization?"
2. Questions exploring concerns. For example: "If I'm hired, I'll report to someone quite a bit younger than me. I believe I'll find this invigorating. Are there potential issues we should discuss?"

- *Learn a bit about what employers may and may not ask in interviews.* Educate yourself, not because you need be on the lookout for discrimination but to help set your expectations and guide your conduct.

- *Be ready to address the reason you're looking for paid work.* Honesty is usually the best policy, but take care in how you describe the situation and your objectives. Avoid sounding desperate, dismissive, or arrogant. Telling potential employers you're broke or bored won't be helpful. Practice talking about this issue in advance with someone still in the workforce. The ideal practice partner is someone in a position that includes interviewing potential employees (because they are well-informed, not necessarily because they might hire you).

- *Determine whether you need a resume and references to apply.* This is something that might have changed since you last looked for work, and it will vary company to company. Create a generic resume, but be prepared to customize both your resume and cover letter for each position you apply for. Create an electronic version of your resume and learn how to submit resumes online, including via email.

Unfortunately, I must also note another change that's taken place in recent years: the lack of response from potential employers. Don't expect a timely confirmation of receipt of your resume, nor a response after interviewing beyond a much belated "You were not selected."

Most employment departments offer free services to help you find and land a job, including support for older persons. The websites for Employment and Social Development Canada (ESDC) and the United States Department of Labor have lots of information and contacts.

Starting Your Own Business

Retirement can be the ideal time to take the leap into starting a business. The options are limitless. A partial list was shown in Part I. Here are some additional businesses that retirees have started:

- Website design
- Landscape/garden design
- Resume writer
- Music or singing teacher
- Medical billing
- Book editing and proofing
- Wardrobe consultant
- Professional organizer
- Life coach
- Speaker
- Caterer or personal chef
- Wedding consultant

Many retirees also enjoy selling their handcrafted items. Avenues for sales include retail shops, craft fairs, flea markets, your own website, and websites such as Etsy that cater to such sales.

The preparation needed to start and run a business varies depending on the nature of the business. However, here are some fundamental pointers that apply to any business:

- *Speak with appropriate advisors about the impact of added income.* Get a clear idea of how much income you may add without negatively affecting taxes and other retirement income and/or benefits. Also discuss the pros and cons of going above that level. Discuss the kinds of things you may and may not deduct as business expenses, as this can affect your finances as well as inform your image of running a business.

- *Research any licenses or permits that might be required.* This includes business licenses, permits to sell certain products, and registration to collect taxes. Ensure you understand what kind of insurance might be required. Don't assume your small or part-time business will be exempt or can operate under the radar. Understanding the elements of overhead cost and the processes you are required to manage—such as sending collected taxes to the appropriate entity—will help you avoid learning things the hard way.

- *Tap into support that can inform and guide your success.* This includes groups offered through your local chambers of commerce, professional associations, and myriad other business groups. Helpful services are available through municipal, provincial/state, or federal organizations.

Things to Watch Out for When Seeking Paid Opportunities

When looking for paid work or a way to launch a business, beware of offers that claim you will make hundreds of dollars an hour, etc. These rarely, if ever, live up to the hype and might even generate serious financial and other problems. If it sounds too good to be true, or like easy money, something is probably suspect about it.

Beware of multilevel marketing (MLM) businesses as well. MLM is also known as pyramid selling, network marketing, and referral marketing. As a guideline, don't enter into a business in which you can only succeed if you recruit others to enter into the same business. If you cannot enjoy at least moderate success by selling the products alone, the business is questionable.

Also exercise caution when jobs or businesses require an upfront investment and/or require you to purchase a certain amount of inventory monthly, quarterly, etc. Although many of these organizations are legitimate and offer terrific ways to operate a small business, it's vital to go into such ventures fully informed. It's okay to consider certain franchise opportunities, especially if the franchiser's outlets, products, or services are well-known and trusted. Long-established and reputable franchisers provide good opportunities because franchising is basically the licensing and support of business models built upon pre-existing and successful formulas.

Whether you start your own fully independent

business or join an organization, look for business ventures that allow you to start small and grow, as this is the most realistic way to build a sustainable business.

Returning to or Completing School

Many retirees choose to attend college, university, or specialty schools. Some do so because they enjoy learning or wish to complete a degree. Many retirees also attend school as a way to start a new career or business.

Research your options in advance, whether you wish to complete a B.A. or a Ph.D., attend an esthetics or culinary school, or become certified as an organizer. There are many benefits beyond business to consider, including those that contribute to a balanced leisure lifestyle.

Unfortunately, due to the recent trend of school recruiters overpromising the value of specific education programs, I must advise you to exercise caution as well. If your primary goal is to increase your income, get estimates of probable income from a third or neutral party rather than the school's staff or recruiters.

Working a Paid Job As an Employee

Goals: By

☐ Receive professional advice and
   guidance on how paid work will
   affect taxes and finances in general.   _____

☐ If applicable: Set employment income
   maximum or range.   _____

☐ Schedule time devoted to job search
   in my calendar.   _____

☐ Land a job.   _____

Additional:

☐ Determine positions for which I'm
   qualified and that are generally
   available in my area.   _____

☐ Identify job-listing resources.   _____

☐ Resume(s) and cover letter(s)
   (including electronic versions) ready.   _____

☐ Ready for interviews.   _____

☐ Networking begun.   _____

☐ _____   _____

☐ _____   _____

☐ _____   _____

Notes:

Working a Paid Job As an Employee (cont'd)

Action Items: **By**

Find out if Joe knows enough about
Social Security to advise me. If not,
find a tax person who can.   Jan 3

_____   _____

_____   _____

_____   _____

_____   _____

_____   _____

_____   _____

_____   _____

_____   _____

_____   _____

_____   _____

_____   _____

_____   _____

_____   _____

_____   _____

_____   _____

Self-Employment

Self-employment includes working as a contractor.

Goals: By

☐ Receive professional advice and
  guidance on how income and business
  expenses will affect taxes and
  finances in general.   _____

☐ If applicable: Set business income
  maximum or range.   _____

☐ Schedule time in calendar devoted to
  researching and/or preparing to
  launch business.   _____

☐ Land first contract or launch business. _____

Additional:

☐ Identify and contact support and
  vendor resources.   _____

☐ Required licenses, permits,
  insurance, etc., ready.   _____

☐ Marketing materials ready (website,
  brochure, resume, etc.)   _____

☐ Marketing plan ready.   _____

☐ Sales skills ready.   _____

☐ _____   _____

☐ _____   _____

☐ _____   _____

Notes:

Self-Employment (cont'd)

Action Items: **By**

Find out if I'll have to charge tax
    on the quilts I sell.   Before the fair

_____   _____

_____   _____

_____   _____

_____   _____

_____   _____

_____   _____

_____   _____

_____   _____

_____   _____

_____   _____

_____   _____

_____   _____

_____   _____

_____   _____

_____   _____

_____   _____

_____   _____

_____   _____

_____   _____

_____   _____

_____   _____

_____   _____

_____   _____

Exploring Volunteering Options

Working as a volunteer provides many benefits, including added structure, opportunities to meet new people, and personal fulfillment. Volunteering also gives us opportunities to develop new skills—skills we might use personally or perhaps eventually use in paid work.

The options for volunteering are many. Rather than list examples in addition to those shown in Part I, here are suggestions for finding opportunities:

- *Look in your mailbox.* You will likely receive solicitation for contributions from organizations that depend on volunteers. Contact the local offices or chapters to inquire.

- *Keep an eye out for charity events.* These are often advertised or announced in the newspaper (as well as in mailers). Many of them occur annually, and you might find good opportunities in planning and/or working at next year's event.

- *Google "volunteer groups" or "volunteer" plus your local area.* You might find a collated list for your area. If not, another area's list might give you ideas for finding local groups.

- *Start with a cause in mind and explore from there.* Would you like to help reduce the feral cat population? Ask local veterinarians about groups or run a focused search on the Internet. Would you like to help schoolchildren in some way? Contact your local school board or, again, run a search on the Internet. Also consider asking if there is a way for you to help out your grandchildren's school.

Manage the Time You Devote to Volunteering

Successfully managing your time is important to enjoying the volunteer experience. As noted in Part I, determine how much time you want to give, and on what schedule, before making a commitment. I recommend you have time frames in mind even before you give an indication of interest or willingness to volunteer. Also, be ready and willing to say no. New volunteers often find themselves bombarded with requests and pleas for their time. At first, this might feel flattering and worthwhile, but it can become burdensome all too quickly.

Manage Your Volunteering Expectations

As most volunteers will tell you, the work can be as challenging as paid work, if not more. The challenges can certainly include the sort we enjoy. For example, the challenge of planning and running a charity golf tournament for the first time might be enjoyable. On the other hand, volunteer organizations often lack adequate guidance for first-timers, which can be an overwhelming and aggravating experience.

Before you jump in, gather information about the work or role as well as the resources, guidance, and support available. Consider the fit for your personality and preferences. Do you enjoy learning as you go or prefer a high level of guidance? Will you be expected to follow past practices even if you want to do something differently?

Also consider the value of stretching yourself—your experiences might provide you with growth far beyond what you had when you worked at paid jobs!

It's also important to consider any organizational politics, especially if you wish to volunteer at a board or committee level. Is there petty infighting or mutual respect? If the former is prevalent, how might that affect your experience in terms of the work or your enjoyment of it? Again, it's often best to avoid jumping right in. Give yourself time to get to know the organization and its leadership, and, as noted above, consider the value of stretching yourself in this area by adding your own leadership to the mix.

The size of volunteer organizations and groups offering volunteer opportunities won't necessarily be relevant. Most national (and international) groups operate using chapters, small subsets of the overall group. Many small and local organizations do excellent work and are very well run. Just keep in mind that every group has its strengths and weaknesses.

Also, almost every organization offers opportunities of various size or scope. For example, your local Habitat for Humanity group would probably welcome you as a volunteer even if you're unable to wield a hammer.

Consider the time you wish to contribute, do your research, and then fold volunteering into your successful retirement.

Volunteering

Goals: **By**

☐ Determine how much time I'm
  open to giving and on what
  schedule.   _____

☐ Create a list of organizations
  with whom I want to consider
  volunteering.   _____

☐ Create list of questions that
  will help me understand the
  role, resources, and
  expectations.   _____

☐ Contact organizations and
  follow up.   _____

☐ Have volunteer work lined up!   _____

☐ _____   _____

☐ _____   _____

☐ _____   _____

Note:

Many successful retirees have shared that they pursued volunteering based on a specific interest—it was one of the goals. Extra spaces are provided so you can do this too.

The goal was often closely related to a balanced leisure lifestyle or one of the success strategies. For example:

I had become somewhat reclusive and made a point to force myself to break the habit. This included purposely volunteering with a group that met weekly for several months. Their expectation that I be there was helpful added pressure.

—Carlos E,. former electrical worker

A gentleman had displayed a large, beautiful nativity in his yard for many years. He had willed that display to the city, but it lay unused and in disrepair for quite some time. When a local group took on restoration and then responsibility for the annual display, I jumped at the chance to help. You see, the original owner of the display was a Sikh, not a Christian. It is my honour to support his legacy of neighbourliness. This is something I would like to be remembered for as well.

—William R., former city worker

Volunteering (cont'd)

Action Items: **By**

Ask Lee about that swim she
does each year. Find out if I'd
have to do a mile!   June

_____   _____

_____   _____

_____   _____

_____   _____

_____   _____

_____   _____

_____   _____

_____   _____

_____   _____

_____   _____

_____   _____

_____   _____

_____   _____

_____   _____

_____   _____

_____   _____

_____   _____

_____   _____

_____   _____

Chapter 19

Applying Chapter 5 (Choosing Where to Live)

Choosing where to live can be complicated, not to mention overwhelming. I strongly recommend you review Chapter 5 before proceeding with working on this portion of your successful retirement vision and plan. The issues are complex because most living situations involve many pros and cons, strengths and weaknesses, and so on. Many of these variables are subjective and even emotional.

Schoolteachers deal with similarly complex issues, and we will borrow one of their tools to help you arrive at a "grade" for the many variables. Just as a teacher assigns grades for math, reading, participation, and comportment, you have the option of assigning a letter grade—A through F—to key components of your living situation.

This will also help bring the planning down to manageable size by dividing the task into three parts:

1. Cost: Clarifying your monthly housing expenses to make budgeting and overall cost considerations easier.

2. Happiness level: Examining intangibles such as how much you like the home and neighbourhood.

3. Future suitability: Considering the suitability of your home as you grow older.

Please note that this chapter does not assume home-ownership. Regardless of your housing situation, you should complete the work and plan. This material also applies to renters and those who room with others.

Tips for Working Through This Chapter

Before you get started, have a look at the following tips, as they should help clarify a few things:

- This part of the planning process applies to your primary residence, not a vacation home. (Work on your vacation home separately, if at all.)

- It's not necessary to complete each part in the order shown, but be sure to complete all three: cost, happiness level, and future suitability.

- I have two suggestions for couples, including housemates:

  1. *Work through the cost portion together.* This applies even when only one person has handled bills and budgeting up to this point.

  2. *Separately work on happiness level and future suitability as a first step.* Working separately makes it easier for each of you to clarify your own thoughts, opinions, and feelings. Once you've done that, discuss your findings and make decisions together.

- If your home has been the "family" home and central gathering place, consider moving gatherings to others' homes from now on. Initiating that change now will make it easier to be objective about your home, and it will enhance your family's ability to carry on beloved (and new) traditions over the long term.

- Don't be afraid to adjust the grading system. There are many ways to grade something, including letter grade A through F, pass or fail, and a scale of 1 through 5 (with either 1 or 5 being the highest). The system used here is a letter grade. If you want to use a different system, just be sure to use the same one for each part. Mixing systems makes it difficult to evaluate your current home on an overall basis. Please also note that giving each key part a grade is optional but recommended.

- Home issues can be distressing. If you find yourself feeling too stressed or overly emotional, back off the process a bit — slow down. If you find yourself feeling overwhelmed, seek help from a trusted friend, spiritual leader, or therapist.

Choosing Where to Live: Summary of Goals and Action Items

The process of choosing where to live is divided into three parts, and each is covered in the following pages. Use this summary to track your progress while completing each part and to help yourself see the issues as a whole. Remember: Assigning grades is optional but recommended.

Goals: **By**

☐ Cost: Calculate and evaluate
   monthly housing expense.   _____

☐ Grade assigned to cost.   Grade: _____

☐ Set cost/expense next steps.   _____

☐ Happiness level: Assess how
   much I/we like our home.   _____

☐ Grade assigned to happiness
   level.   Grade: _____

☐ Set any next steps.   _____

☐ Future suitability: Evaluate
   my/our home's suitability
   as we age.   _____

☐ Grade assigned to future
   suitability.   Grade: _____

☐ Set any next steps.   _____

As applicable:

☐ My/our home's overall grade.   Grade: _____

☐ Set a target time frame to find
   a new home.   That time is: _____

☐ Create an action plan for
finding a new home. _____
☐ Set a time to re-evaluate
my/our home. That time is: _____
☐ _____ _____
☐ _____ _____
☐ _____ _____
☐ _____ _____
☐ _____ _____
☐ _____ _____
☐ _____ _____
☐ _____ _____
☐ _____ _____

Choosing Where to Live: Cost

The primary objective for this exercise is to determine whether it's advisable to find a less expensive home, either now or at some point in the future. There are two things to do to reach this objective:

1. Determine the monthly cost of your home.

2. Work with a CPA, financial planner, or similar advisor to grade your home's expense/cost.

Working with a professional is recommended because simple math alone won't provide an accurate evaluation. There are many ways to determine a grade. You can use the letter grade system as introduced above, but rely on your advisor for guidance according to your unique situation. In other words, use whatever evaluation system your advisor recommends.

The following pages provide tips for calculating monthly home expenses and determining your home's grade in terms of cost. The goals and action items sheet is provided at the end of this section.

Calculating Your Monthly Home Cost

A worksheet is provided below for your convenience. Many of the following tips refer to an item in the worksheet, so you might want to make a copy to have it handy for reference.

- *Rent*. This is usually straightforward because it's paid monthly, but factor in an appropriate added percentage if rent increases regularly.

- *Adjustable rate mortgages.* If your monthly payment varies, use the highest possible amount in your calculation.

- *Mortgage lines of credit.* It might be best to assume that the line of credit is maxed out and use the applicable monthly payment. As noted above, use the higher payment if the rate or amount varies.

- *Homeowners' association fees, community fees, and similar fees.* Be sure to include these fees, even if they're relatively modest.

- *Homeowners' association or community assessments.* Homeowner organizations occasionally charge members an amount above and beyond monthly payments. It's best to assume this will occur unless you have very good reason to believe it won't. Use the highest assessment amount from the past five years, dividing it by twelve to get a monthly amount. If no assessment has occurred, use your best guess.

- *Property taxes.* Divide the total annual bill by twelve to get a monthly amount. If you also pay parcel taxes or other amounts linked to property ownership, determine the monthly amount and include it in the total.

- *Subtotal of mortgage, homeowners' dues, and taxes if you're a homeowner, or rent amount if you're a renter.*

It's important to confer with an expert—a CPA or financial advisor—to see if your housing expenses are considered reasonable, relatively high, or comfortably low. Many of these experts will focus on the cost shown in this subtotal.

- *Insurance*. Determine a monthly amount for homeowners or renters insurance as well as an amount for fire, flood, earthquake, or other insurance linked to your home. Have insurance rates been increasing? Factor in a higher amount to allow a more accurate picture of home cost. Is your homeowners insurance or other insurance included as part of the homeowners' association due payments? There's no need to show this separately if it's included elsewhere.

- *Utilities*. Include electricity, water, gas, and garbage/recycling pickup. List each on a separate line if you wish, or simply show a total. Utility bills tend to vary. Take last year's total and divide it by twelve. (Are rates due to increase?) Factor in a reasonable amount so you have an accurate picture of this expense.

- *Other*. Add any other housing expenses to your calculation. These might include the following:

  1. Housecleaner/housekeeper
  2. Gardener, pool maintenance, septic maintenance, or other maintenance (if used regularly)
  3. Pest control, gutter cleaning, snow removal, etc.

Calculate the annual cost of these, including the usual gratuities, and divide it by twelve to get a monthly amount. Remember to include any monthly fees for alarm services and other regular expenses linked specifically to your home.

- *Subtotal of insurance, utilities, and all other expenses.* This amount might be useful for analysis too.

- *Grand total of all monthly home expenses.*

Don't include the following expenses in the above cost calculation: food, cable or satellite TV services, Internet, and phones. However, an advisor might want this information to help you arrive at a grade for cost. (Regardless, these expenses should be included in your overall budget.)

If you have a home-based business or you rent out a portion of your home or property, don't subtract any tax-deductible amounts, such as for a home office. Doing so will make the cost calculation inaccurate. Talk with your advisor about how to handle cost and income from any rental.

Monthly Home Cost

Rent or Mortgage Expense:

Rent or first mortgage payment $_____

Second and any other mortgage $_____

Homeowners' Association, etc:

Homeowners', community, or
      other similar dues $_____

Related assessment cost $_____

Taxes:

Property tax, parcel taxes, etc. $_____

Subtotal A $_____

Insurance:

Homeowners or renters $_____

Fire, flood, earthquake or other $_____

Utilities: Total of electricity,
      water, gas, garbage, etc. $_____

Other:

Housecleaner/housekeeper $_____

Gardener, pool maintenance,
      septic maintenance, etc. $_____

Pest control, gutter cleaning, snow
      removal, etc. $_____

Alarm system $\underline{\hspace{2cm}}$

Other: $\underline{\hspace{3cm}}$ $\$\underline{\hspace{2cm}}$

Other: $\underline{\hspace{3cm}}$ $\$\underline{\hspace{2cm}}$

Other: $\underline{\hspace{3cm}}$ $\$\underline{\hspace{2cm}}$

Subtotal B $\$\underline{\hspace{2cm}}$

Grand total (A + B) $\$\underline{\hspace{2cm}}$

Grading Your Home's Cost

The grand total cost is only a dollar figure. Consult with a professional, such as a CPA or financial planner, to determine a grade for your home based on that monthly cost. The grading system shown below is an example. You or your advisor should feel free to alter the definitions or use another system entirely.

A Grade

- The cost is relatively low. Paying home costs does not require you to use more income and savings than is advisable.
- You have room to handle financial emergencies and/or new expenses for things such as in-home care for an extended period.

B Grade

- The cost is relatively low. Paying home costs does not require you to use more income and savings than is advisable.
- You have room to handle financial emergencies and/or new expenses for things such as in-home care for up to two years.

C Grade

- The cost is neither relatively low nor relatively high. Paying home costs might require you to use slightly more income and savings than is advisable.
- You have room to handle financial emergencies and/or new expenses for things such as in-home care on a limited basis (one year or less).

D Grade

- The cost is relatively high and requires you to use more income and savings than is advisable.
- Should a financial emergency arise or new expenses be added, you will have to add debt (including using credit cards and/or lines of credit).

F Grade

- The cost is far higher than recommended and requires you to use far more income and savings than is advisable.
- Should a financial emergency arise or new expenses be added, your financial situation will grow markedly worse.

Grading Your Home's Cost: What's Next?

- Use the goals and action items sheet below to note the grade given to cost as well as to track progress toward other cost-related goals. Also note the completion, grade, etc., on the summary sheet provided at the beginning of this chapter.

- A poor grade for home cost (D or F) does not necessarily mean one should find a less expensive home as soon as possible. Options to better the situation might include reducing debt or other expenses, or buying long-term care insurance. Again, it's important to work with experts on such issues. Talk with your advisors, and do your best to apply their advice.

You can potentially use the time frames in the example grading system to guide future actions as needed. For example:

> Bob and Cheryl worked with their CPA using the grading system introduced in this chapter. Their current home was graded a "B," in part because they would be able to handle added expenses for up to two years.
>
> Sometime later, Cheryl began to experience health problems. Bob and Cheryl decided to hire a general household helper for Cheryl. After consulting with their advisor, and with the grading time frame of two years in mind, Bob and Cheryl made the following decisions:
>
> 1. If the added expense of a household helper continues at the same level, they will begin to look for a new home in one year, which will give them an additional year to move to a new home.
>
> 2. If expenses increase, they will move the timeline up six months.
>
> Bob and Cheryl also engaged their advisor in keeping to this plan. Their advisor agreed to check in regularly and remind them of their commitment as appropriate.

Home Cost

Remember that cost is just one element to consider. Use the summary sheet to note all three.

Goals: **By**

☐ Calculate cost per month.   _____

☐ Confer with advisor(s) to grade home on
    its cost.   **Grade:**   _____

As applicable:

☐ Implement expense cutting for current home.   _____

☐ Receive a cost guideline for a new home.   _____

☐ Define other next steps.   _____

Action Items: **By**

Itemize home expenses for
last three months (i.e., mortgage,
property taxes, heat, water,
electricity). Discuss costs
with Jim, our CPA.   *July / August*

_____   _____

_____   _____

_____   _____

_____   _____

_____   _____

_____   _____

Choosing Where to Live: Happiness Level

Do I like where I now live, or am I simply used to it? Good question!
—Peter B., writer

It can be surprisingly difficult to determine if you're happy with your home for a few reasons. The first reason is the high level of comfort that often comes with living in the same place for years. We grow accustomed to the doors that stick every winter. We hardly notice the limited closet space. Familiarity makes it difficult to separate things we like from things we find comfortable.

In addition, negative changes to our home and neighbourhood often happen slowly enough that we simply adapt to them. We drive around the potholes without thinking and don't notice the noise of the now busy street unless someone brings it to our attention.

Adaptation also includes taking things on balance. Being able to observe fawns in our backyard might be worth having grown deer eat the flowers. Those heavily tattooed kids down the block might have at first given us pause, but they also shovel our walk now and then.

Of course, we often have strong sentimental attachments to our home. Family photos hang on its walls. Doorways have dings where the kids and grandkids banged into them. Certain neighbours might have moved away, but we still fondly remember barbeques shared in the backyard.

All of the above might just as easily describe why you're genuinely happy with your home! This exercise will help you determine if familiarity, adaptation, and fond memories are strong contributors to your satisfaction and happiness—or if they're simply holding you back.

As with the cost evaluation, the goals here include grading the happiness element. However, don't be concerned if you're unable to determine a grade, or if you and your partner cannot agree on a grade. You're in good company: Philosophers have struggled to define happiness for years! Regardless, I recommend making the effort to work through the exercise whether you arrive at a grade or not. The process itself might prove extremely useful.

Evaluating home happiness isn't just for homeowners. Complete this exercise whether you own or rent your home. Homeowners might want to put extra consideration toward things such as being fully responsible for upkeep, increasing expenses, and so on. Renters might want to put extra consideration toward things such as less ability to make changes to the home, any concerns about increasing rent, or concerns about being forced to move.

Determining Your Home Happiness Level
"Home" can include the dwelling, its parts, and the neighbourhood. A worksheet showing these elements is provided below for your convenience. "Home" can also include the larger area in which we live and the associated elements, including the greater metropolitan or rural area, the province or state, tax levels, politics, environmental issues, etc. Use the blank spots on the worksheet to add these into the exercise if you wish.

Although you can certainly choose your own definitions (or another system entirely), here are suggestions for defining the letter grades for this exercise:

- A = Consistently happy with my home
- B = Mostly and/or often happy with my home
- C = Satisfied and not unhappy with my home
- D = Somewhat unhappy and/or often unhappy with my home
- F = Not happy and/or often very unhappy with my home

Tips for Determining Your Happiness Level

- If you're part of a couple, you both should first work through the exercise individually. When you come together to talk things over, it's not necessary for both of you to determine a grade or agree on the same grade. It *is* important that each person be heard and that you decide how to move forward together.

- Not happy with the word *happiness*? If it doesn't resonate with you, try using words or phrases that include words such as *content*, *pleased*, or *enjoyable*. As for *unhappy*, this includes feeling frustrated, worried, unsafe, irritated, stressed, etc.

- Try to grade your home as a whole first. If that doesn't work well, consider its parts—or any parts you consider important—and use the results to choose an overall grade. However, remember that it's not vital to arrive at a grade at all.

- Some experts suggest that using snap judgments—choosing without giving yourself time to think about it—is most illustrative of your real feelings. You would apply this theory here by quickly choosing a grade for your home as a whole (or for each part of your home). Other experts, however, suggest the opposite. They recommend giving yourself time and space to reflect or meditate on the issue. Which is better? Use the method that most appeals to you, or experiment with both.

- One way to evaluate your home is to compare it to other homes you know fairly well. Are there things you like about your friends' homes? It can be helpful to talk about what you like with the homeowner because sometimes there are negatives that only they are aware of. For example, you might like the hot tub in your neighbour's backyard but lack information about its associated utility cost.

- Going to open houses in homes for sale might help you see your own home more objectively. Visiting open houses can also clarify how open you are to moving or remodelling. However, don't insist your partner accompany you if they don't enjoy looking at open houses.

- Evaluating your home's strengths and weaknesses, and what you would have to do to your home to position it for sale, can be informative. Ask for a professional's input on this, preferably a friend in real estate. Don't impose on a realtor if you have no intention of putting your home on the market.

- If you're stuck and unable to clarify how happy you are with your current home, or if you and your partner disagree, determine whether you're open to considering a new home or remodelling your current home if that's feasible.

A Few More Words on the Exercise and Worksheets

- Individual goals are designed for everyone, whether you're part of a couple or not.

- Couples: Make copies of the blank worksheets. Each of you should have your own set. You'll also need another set to use as a couple. Meet the individual goals first, and work on meeting the couples goals second.

- As mentioned above, the process of consideration is more important than determining a grade.

- If you use a grading system, remember to use the same system for all three elements: cost, happiness level, and future suitability (e.g., use letter grades for all three).

- The goals for the happiness level exercise include remodelling as an option. Be sure to consult with your financial advisor and real estate professional to determine whether remodelling is advisable.

Grading Your Home's Happiness Level

Home _____   Grade Overall _____

Example Grade Definitions:

A: Completely and consistently happy

B: Mostly and/or often happy

C: Satisfied and not unhappy

D: Somewhat unhappy and/or often unhappy

F: Not happy and/or often very unhappy

Kitchen	_____	Dining room	_____
Master bedroom	_____	Master bath	_____
Closets/storage	_____	Living room	_____
Family room	_____	Other bed.	_____
Other bathrooms	_____	Garage	_____
Front yard	_____	Backyard	_____
Balconies/patios	_____	Attic	_____
Basement	_____	Guests room	_____
Laundry	_____	Plumb/heat/AC	_____
Transportation	_____	Traffic	_____
Safety	_____	Parking	_____
Upkeep	_____	Landlord	_____
Urban or rural area	_____	Neighbourhood	_____

Homeowners' Assoc. or similar   _____

Common areas (pool, gym)   _____

Environment (allergens, noise)   _____

Services (e.g., doorman)   _____

Use this space to add and grade other elements:

Home Happiness Level

Goals for individuals :   **By**

☐ Work through exercise.   _____

☐ Schedule and complete any activities
   to clarify my feelings or grade.   _____

☐ Select my personal happiness grade
   for my/our home.   _____

                              Grade: _____

☐ Alternate: Determine openness to
   considering a new home or
   remodelling if it's feasible.   _____

Notes:

Additional Goals for Couples :   **By**

☐ Discuss thoughts or results of exercise.   _____

☐ Schedule and complete any activities to
   help resolve any issues.   _____

☐ Choose a joint grade or determine
   openness to considering a new home
   or remodelling if it's feasible.   _____

                              Grade: _____

☐ Determine any next steps.   _____

Notes:

**Remember to also note goals and grades on the summary
sheet at the beginning of this chapter.**

Home Happiness Level (cont'd)

Action Items: **By**

*Ask Claudia to tell us what we'd
have to do to make our home more
attractive for sale. Talk with Sam
about remodelling the kitchen and
adding a bedroom.*   *May*

_____   _____

_____   _____

_____   _____

_____   _____

_____   _____

_____   _____

_____   _____

_____   _____

_____   _____

_____   _____

_____   _____

_____   _____

_____   _____

_____   _____

_____   _____

_____   _____

_____   _____

Notes:

Choosing Where to Live: Future Suitability

In this section, you will evaluate how suitable your home will be over time as you grow older. To complete the exercise, you'll need to imagine yourself and/or your significant other as being less physically able than you are now. Of course, *older* and *less physically able* are relative terms, and determining what they mean is an individual matter. Are you older five years from now? Ten? If you're less able to walk up and down steps in fifteen years, will you simply be tired of the necessity or glad to exercise your leg muscles?

Although we cannot accurately predict the future—including our future attitudes—this exercise will help you consider practical matters you can accurately forecast, including the following:

- How difficult would it be to live in your home if you were to become less physically able or impaired in some way? For example, does the building have an elevator that works reliably? Do you have at least one bedroom and bathroom on the ground floor of your home?

- How easy would it be to alter your home to suit different physical needs? For example, could a stair lift be added? Could you add a bedroom and/or bathroom on the ground floor?

- How would making accommodations affect your financial situation? For example, would you likely need to use savings and/or add debt?

This exercise focuses on evaluating your home's suitability in the future. If your health is very good, you might instead choose a point in the future to complete the exercise, such as one, three, or five years from now. Engage your advisor, a friend, or a family member to hold you to that so you follow through with it.

Tips for Evaluating Your Home's Future Suitability

- As odd as it might sound, one of the best times to complete this exercise is when you're feeling under the weather—down with a bad cold or flu, for example. When you're congested and feel achy, it's easier to imagine being less willing or able to go up and down stairs several times a day!

- You might find it helpful to involve a friend or family member. They can help evaluate your home more objectively, help brainstorm potential options, and help complete your research.

- Don't assume that you or your partner will be able to take care of the other person. For this exercise, assume you will both be equally in need.

- Don't let the idea of being "old" get in the way of making practical changes now. Small things, such as adding non-slip strips in the tub or a handrail by the back steps, can be good additions at any age.

Things to Evaluate for Future Suitability
You should evaluate the following as applicable:

- Is your home easy to maintain inside and out? If not, would assistance be affordable?

- Can you easily add handrails near toilets and in showers and tubs? Installation might take certain expertise. Would you easily afford the cost for installation?

- Are there steps to get in and out of your home, including from the garage, lobby, laundry room, etc.? Are there handrails by all steps, or could they be added? Would ramps be feasible if needed? It's easy to forget that even one or two steps are still steps—these count!

- Does your home have more than one floor? Would it be possible to live on the ground floor (or on the floor most easily accessible)? Would it be feasible and affordable to install a stair lift? How about remodelling to add a bedroom and bathroom?

- Does the driveway, yard, sidewalks, etc., have steep inclines? Are there steps and/or handrails to make going up and down safer and easier? If not, could they be added affordably?

- What are the transportation options if you no longer drive? Are the options affordable?

- Is there a grocery store within easy—perhaps walking or wheeling—distance? How about a library, senior centre, park, and so on? Are those places wheelchair/ walker accessible?

- Do doorways have obstacles such as raised casements for sliding glass doors and thresholds for entry doors? If so, can you afford to install ramps for these if needed?

- If there are elevators in your building, are they reliable? Could you get downstairs in an emergency such as an earthquake or fire? If you needed help, would neighbours be available and able to assist? (i.e., Do most of your neighbours work during the day?)

- Do you live in an area that gets very cold and/or hot? If so, would you be okay if the electricity went out? Could you get to a shelter if needed? Are such shelters commonly made available?

- Is there convenient access to medical and dental care? How about emergency care?

- Do you have friends or family within a thirty-minute drive who could—and probably would—help from time to time? (Thirty minutes is an arbitrary number, so adjust as appropriate.)

- If you or your partner were using a wheelchair, would it be easy to maneuver through the home, including the kitchen and at least one full bathroom? How wide are the doorways and hallways? Experts suggest minimum width of thirty-two inches, or thirty-six inches if a turn is involved. If your home will not easily accommodate adjustments for wheelchair use, it does not necessarily mean a low grade is warranted. Consider any health issues and financial ability to quickly find a new home should such needs arise.

- If there were need for twenty-four-hour care, would there be a place for caregivers to sleep? This need not be a separate bedroom; a sofa bed or daybed often suffices.

- Do you enjoy your home enough that spending a lot of time there would be pleasant? If not, this suggests that finding a new home is a good idea.

Grading Your Home's Future Suitability

The example shown below focuses on making adjustments to your current home should the need arise. Alter the definitions if you wish! (If you use a different grading system, remember to use the same system for other exercises in this chapter.)

A   Very few minor adjustments likely to be needed.
B   Easy and inexpensive to make almost any needed adjustments.
C   Most adjustments could be made, and expenses are likely manageable.
D   Most adjustments could be made, but expenses would likely hurt financial situation. Or: Minor adjustments could be made but not major adjustments.
F   Most adjustments would be difficult or impossible to make and/or unaffordable.

What to Do with a C or Lower Grade on Future Suitability

Every situation is different, and future suitability is just one of three aspects for evaluating where you live. However, the following suggestions and comments might be helpful:

- Multilevel homes with a bedroom and bathroom on the ground floor are often desirable. Consult with financial and real estate professionals to determine whether this kind of remodelling would be a good investment even if you choose to sell your home in the future.

- If your home's future suitability gets a D or F grade and your health is good, choose a time in the future to re-evaluate your home and situation, such as one, three, or five years from now. Engage your advisor, a friend, or a family member to hold you to that so you follow through with it.

- If your home's future suitability gets a D or F grade and your and/or your partner's health is not good, please don't merely hope the situation improves; take steps now to find a home that will be enjoyable and safe for years to come.

Future Suitability of Your Home

Goals: By
☐ Work through exercise.   _____
☐ Schedule and complete any action
   items to inform grade.   _____
☐ Select future suitability grade for
   my/our home.   _____
                                    Grade: _____

As applicable:
☐ Explore possible remodelling and
   make a decision whether to do it.   _____
☐ Create a list of adjustments and plan
   of action to complete them.   _____
☐ Set time to evaluate or re-evaluate
   home (Date: _____)   _____
☐ Engage someone to hold me/us to
   the above. (Name: _____)   _____
☐ _____   _____
☐ _____   _____
☐ _____   _____
Notes:

Remember to also note goals and grades on the summary
sheet at the beginning of this chapter.

Future Suitability of Your Home (cont'd)

Action Items: **By**

Add a handrail to the front steps.   Oct 1

_____   _____

_____   _____

_____   _____

_____   _____

_____   _____

_____   _____

_____   _____

_____   _____

_____   _____

_____   _____

_____   _____

_____   _____

_____   _____

_____   _____

_____   _____

_____   _____

_____   _____

_____   _____

_____   _____

_____   _____

_____   _____

_____   _____

Worksheet:

Use this blank sheet to make copies for any of the above exercises.

Goals: By

☐ _____   _____
☐ _____   _____
☐ _____   _____
☐ _____   _____
☐ _____   _____
☐ _____   _____

Action Items: By

_____   _____
_____   _____
_____   _____
_____   _____
_____   _____
_____   _____
_____   _____
_____   _____
_____   _____
_____   _____
_____   _____
_____   _____
_____   _____
_____   _____
_____   _____
_____   _____

Chapter 20

Applying Chapter 6 (Developing Personal Traits for Success)

Those of us who tend to dwell on the negative often find retirement extremely challenging. However, even if we have a positive attitude and strong spirituality, retirement presents new challenges.

It's clear that attitude, mental health, and spirituality often make the difference between a successful and an unsuccessful retirement. In this chapter, we will focus on how we can choose a positive attitude, take steps to improve our health, and proactively feed our spirit. How we do this is individual and quite personal, so below are blank worksheets for goals and action items, ready for you to fill in as you wish.

Tips for Developing Personal Traits for Success
This exercise involves introspection and self-discovery. The following tips will help you get started:

* This section covers very personal matters. If you have concerns about privacy, use a separate notebook or journal for notes, tracking action items, etc. If you want even better protection, consider using a word processing program such as Microsoft Word and add password protection to the document file. Alternatively, simply ensure that your computer itself requires

a password for access.

- Few of us accurately recognize our own weaknesses (and often our strengths too). Enlisting a professional or someone you trust might help you clarify areas you need to work on. Self-help books and other resources that include self-assessment tools can also be very helpful.

- Developing a successful retirement is not necessarily a linear process. You might need to work on these issues more than once. Don't worry. This is normal!

- We have many options for strengthening our positive attitudes, mental health, and spirituality, including working with therapists, life coaches, and spiritual advisors. We can also grow through participation in activities such as drum circles, activities sponsored by places of worship, support groups, and meditation classes—to name just a few options.

- Having many options can be wonderful, but you should exercise some caution. Be especially cautious about individuals, organizations, products, or services that require you to spend a lot of money to reap the "rewards" of their assistance.

Developing and Strengthening Positive Attitudes
Some people adopt negative attitudes about retirement, sometimes without even realizing it. They fall into negative thinking by believing their best days are behind them.

Such negative thinking coupled with passive responses to challenges almost inevitably leads to a loss of zest for life and deteriorated health. Even people with innate positive attitudes about life can experience fear, panic, and discomfort when planning for or entering retirement. These are normal reactions to entering a new world filled with significantly different circumstances. It's what you do from there that's most important.

Our attitudes, whether positive or negative, are based on emotional and mental habits. The more we think in negative ways, the more ingrained negative attitudes become. The opposite is true as well: We can practice the art of positive thinking to develop and strengthen positive attitudes.

Below are pointers for developing positive attitudes, even in the face of challenges common to retirement. As you read through them, try treating them as a sort of self-assessment: Is this already a personal strength or is it something you need or want to work on?

Stay in the Present

It's natural to think about your past, including your career. It's one thing to recognize mistakes or things you didn't accomplish, but it's quite another to dwell on them until you become stuck in the past. If you find yourself repeatedly thinking about your past in a negative way, redirect your focus to the present. Start by asking yourself this question: "What will I do now to influence my present and future?" Next, answer the question and follow through with action!

Take Ownership

As noted above, almost everyone encounters challenges when planning for or entering retirement. These challenges can feel overwhelming, and you might not always immediately overcome them. When you run into problems or when you feel discouraged, ask yourself the following question: "What do I need to do to bring about the changes I want?" You might also need to bring the challenge down to size: "What small step will get me started on making that change?" Next, answer the question(s) and follow through with action.

Other ownership issues arise when we want another person to change so that *our* life will change in some way. It's important to get professional help if it's a serious issue (e.g., your partner is abusing alcohol). However, wanting another person to change quite often means little things such as leaving wet towels on the floor or donating favourite sweatshirts to charity without permission. The way we think about the desired changes affects our attitudes. The more we focus on what we can do ourselves, the more positive we tend to feel about the situation.

It often takes just a slight alteration in thought to feed a positive attitude and improve our ability to communicate. For example, "My wife, Sarah, should go on walks with me more often" becomes "I will tell my wife how much I enjoy walking with her and ask how often she's willing to go walking with me" or perhaps "I'll tell my wife how much I enjoy walking with her, continue to ask her to go, and see what happens." And if your wife doesn't want to go on those walks? Take those walks yourself and/or find something Sarah does want to do with you.

Surround Yourself with Positive People

Surrounding yourself with positive people helps you feel positive too. In addition to taking steps to find and nurture relationships with those folks, you might also need to change or exit existing relationships with negative people. The following are some common examples:

- Do long-time friends focus conversations on the past, especially past careers? Create new things to talk about by sharing new activities that provide a topic, such as going to museums, taking a class together, seeing movies or plays, etc.

- Do negative people seem to gravitate to you? Don't encourage a new acquaintance's negativity in an effort to be friendly. You need not be unsympathetic. Instead, after listening for a time, ask questions such as "And what are you doing for fun?" You can also gently turn the conversation to yourself and talk in positive terms about your life. They will either come around or find someone else to talk with.

- People sometimes adopt negative attitudes as a way to support a friendship. Many of us do this unintentionally; in fact, we might not even recognize how often we put a negative spin on things. For example, in a lighthearted tone of voice, we might say, "Traffic was terrible, and it took forever to find a parking space, but we finally found a great one right by the stairwell," or, "I heard the movie is great, but can you believe the price of popcorn…?" These mixed messages not only downplay the positive; they also make your life seem and feel overly complicated. If this sounds a bit like you, force yourself to leave the negative things unsaid. Simply let people know that you found a nice parking space and that you heard the movie is terrific and can't wait to see it.

- If you're working on developing positive attitudes—and if you were previously negative—be aware that your friends might themselves have adopted a somewhat negative or pessimistic stance in response to their interactions with you. Changing the kinds of things you do together and talking positively yourself can break this pattern in a good way. Be persistent and give things time to change, as old habits take a while to fade. If the pattern doesn't change with certain people, consider seeing them less often.

Remove Yourself from the Centre

People with negative attitudes often see themselves as being the centre of the universe and take things personally. One of the ways to recognize this in ourselves is to consider how often we blow minor irritants out of proportion. For example, if the young clerk at the store doesn't call you "sir," do you see it as personal slight? Did that driver ahead of you this morning purposely drive slowly to make you late?

A self-focused perspective makes us very difficult to be around. Making mountains out of molehills also affects our ability to handle the truly challenging issues in life. Volunteering—doing things for others—is one of the best ways to remove yourself from the centre of the universe and gain an appropriate perspective.

General Tips for Developing and Strengthening Positive Attitudes

The following tips will help you develop and strengthen positive attitudes. However, also be sure to see the section below that covers mental and physical health, as it will help as well.

- Lighten up! People with positive attitudes see humour in situations. The next time you or your partner spills ground coffee all over the floor, practice having a good laugh over it. Watching funny movies regularly can also strengthen your ability to let the little things go.

- Find and listen to your own personal theme song. Many athletes, professional speakers, and others have an uplifting or energizing song they listen to as part of their preparation for an event. You can do the same. Find a song for yourself that you can listen to as you begin your day or whenever you need an extra boost.

- Affirmations and some forms of meditation essentially bring positive images and self-talk to mind at will. This practice develops a more positive and resilient mindset overall. You can learn the art of affirmations and meditation through classes, books, audiobooks, and videos. Use these to receive instruction and practice in having positive attitudes! Note that some forms of meditation work on "clearing your mind." Steer away from these, as meditation shouldn't simply involve "zoning out." Look for meditation that involves filling your mind with positive imagery and thoughts.

- Having positive attitudes—engaging in positive self-talk—includes believing you deserve love and a successful retirement. Affirmations can be especially helpful in overcoming self-doubt in these areas. People who work on quieting self-doubt often find early efforts at affirmations bring up deep emotion and tears. Please don't let this dissuade you from continuing the practice, as this is evidence you are clearing out baggage!

- Many of us are most vulnerable to negative thinking when we first wake up in the morning. If you tend to wake with worry and/or negative thoughts, don't just lie there mulling things over or considering your day to come. Force yourself to get out of bed quickly and get moving.

- As the saying goes, count your blessings. The simple act of recognizing the positives in your life, both big and small, is important for developing and strengthening positive attitudes. Many people find this activity is a great way to start the day on the right foot.

- Saying things aloud often has more impact than only thinking them. Speaking your affirmations aloud, singing along to your theme song, and saying hello to your day with a smile on your face are all examples of little things that can make a big difference. The activity of speaking sends stronger signals to your brain and throughout your body, so you will learn positive attitudes and feel the effects more quickly.

Developing and Strengthening Positive Attitudes

Goals: **By**

☐ *Say affirmations daily with*
   morning coffee.   *Now*

☐ _____   _____

☐ _____   _____

☐ _____   _____

☐ _____   _____

☐ _____   _____

☐ _____   _____

Action Items: **By**

Reread " How to Make Friends and
Influence People" by Dale Carnegie   *June*

_____   _____

_____   _____

_____   _____

_____   _____

_____   _____

_____   _____

_____   _____

_____   _____

_____   _____

_____   _____

_____   _____

_____   _____

_____   _____

Developing and Maintaining Good Mental and Physical Health

The changes associated with retirement can generate physical symptoms such as sweaty palms, butterflies in the stomach, general anxiety, nausea, and insomnia. Many people experience these feelings upon entering retirement, but we can certainly experience these symptoms at any time.

It's normal to feel stress and distress. This section includes tips you can apply any time you experience symptoms. You can also apply them every day to improve mental and physical health. As you read through this section, use the content to identify things you want to work on to improve your mental and physical health.

Symptoms of Stress Overload

Consult with your doctor if you have one or more of the symptoms below:

• Headaches	• Numerous colds, cold sores, and other viral disorders
• Skin rashes	• Ulcers or digestive problems
• Irritability	• A feeling of your heart racing, or palpitations
• Insomnia	• Accidental injury due to inattention or distraction

Should you try stress relievers before seeing your doctor? It's usually best to consult with your doctor early to discuss your plans and/or activities.

Stress Relievers

The following activities will help reduce stress:

- *Engage in regular physical exercise, daily if possible.* This is also a key component of a balanced leisure lifestyle. Regular physical exercise is an excellent stress reliever. Walking, swimming, playing golf, using the gym or home gym, and dancing are all ways to reduce or eliminate stress.

- *Practice yoga or t'ai chi ch'uan (tai chi).* These physical exercises have an added benefit of relaxation and are therefore great for reducing stress. Both can also improve balance, which is an issue for many of us as we grow older.

- *Use deep breathing, including as part of meditation.* Take a deep breath in through your nose. Hold it for ten seconds and then release it slowly through your mouth. Repeat for five minutes. This not only relieves stress; it can also help lower your heart rate and blood pressure.

- *Use progressive muscle relaxation.* This is fully described in Chapter 6. The method generally focuses relaxation from your feet, up through your body, to your head. You can use this method anywhere you can stretch out and relax. But be advised that it can be so relaxing that you'll fall asleep!

- *Use visualization.* Using visualization as a relaxation technique is also described in Chapter 6. The type of visualization you'll want to use involves picturing a place where you feel happy, safe, relaxed, and comfortable. You can use a similar technique to visualize your successful retirement, but that type of visualization is intended to be creative and energizing.

- *Talk things out and get help from others.* We all need sympathy, understanding, and support. We also need information, encouragement, and advice. Seeking input and help from friends, family, and professionals can be vital to relieving stress and moving forward. This includes consulting with your doctor.

- *Slow things down.* Making the transition to retirement often involves sharp and abrupt changes. In addition, some of us are prone to hurrying in an effort to get past unpleasant things. If you find yourself feeling stressed, or if the decisions you're making feel forced, consider slowing the process down if you can. Another way to reduce stress in these cases is to make smaller changes that involve smaller decisions. This is not to say you should put planning and implementation completely aside. Momentum can be difficult to regain, so it's best to keep moving forward at least a little bit at a time. The more active you are in choosing your path and following through, the more satisfied you'll be.

- *Combat the blues.* Below are for tips for picking yourself up when the blues get you down.

Tips for Combating the Blues

Feeling the holiday blues (Make plans in advance if you often feel this way)	• Invite a friend to do something with you (rather than waiting to be invited). • Volunteer at a shelter, deliver meals to shut-ins, etc. • See a movie on the key day of the holiday. • Go on a special cruise (if affordable).
Feeling sorry for yourself and/or resenting others	• Watch a comedy. • Watch a very sad movie and have a "good" cry. • Make an effort to identify the positives in your life. • Volunteer to help those less fortunate than you.
Dreading weekends	• Increase your weekend activities, including making plans in advance with friends.
Feeling generally anxious	• Speak with a confidant. (Speak with a professional if the anxiety does not abate.)
Feeling lonely	• Proactively invite friends to do something with you. • Add a pet to your life. • Work harder on finding a group or club to join.
Experiencing the winter blues	• Engage in a winter-specific activity (e.g., skating).

	• Look into light therapy (or phototherapy).
Worried over finances	• Talk things over with your financial advisor.
	• Make needed changes, even if they're small.
Dislike being alone at night	• Add a pet to your life.
	• Consider moving to a retirement community.
	• Consider a housemate or roommate.
	• Add an alarm system if you're worried about safety.
Feeling lethargic, sleeping "too much," or experiencing insomnia	• Get more physical exercise, including taking regular walks.
	• Add a short afternoon nap to your routine.
	• See your doctor.
Turning to alcohol or drugs for a pick-me-up	• Speak with a counsellor, such as clergy and senior centre advisors.
Feeling uncomfortable with a more relaxed routine	• Tell yourself you're worth it!

Keeping Your Brain Stimulated

Maintaining good health also means keeping your brain active and challenged. As we age, we need to pay extra attention to keeping our brain cells working! Here's a list of tips for assisting your brain cells and increasing your brain health:

- Work on brainteasers, logic problems, word games, and puzzles.
- Play board games that require strategic thinking, such chess and checkers.
- Do math without a calculator.
- Use your non-dominant hand for activities such as brushing your teeth or moving a computer mouse.
- Visualize, spell, pronounce, and write words backwards.
- Take up juggling.
- Attend debates and lectures.
- Take classes, including online classes.
- Teach.
- Learn to play a musical instrument.
- Play 3-D video games that require spatial orientation, hand–eye coordination, and/or memory recall.
- Take a creative writing class.
- Memorize lists.
- Learn a foreign language.
- Read a book or magazine instead of watching TV.
- If you're in the habit of reading with the TV on, turn the TV off.
- Go through the grocery store in reverse (i.e., start on the left of the store if you usually start on the right).

- Take up a hobby or craft that requires greater thought or concentration. Although this can apply to almost anything new, crafts that require building or calculations are especially effective (e.g., woodworking or quilting).
- Write letters by hand.
- Research your ancestry and create a way to show your family tree (rather than letting a website's program do it for you).
- Watch TV or movies without closed captions.

Developing and Maintaining Good Mental and Physical Health

Goals: **By**

☐ *Have an activity ready for*
    Thanksgiving weekend.   *Oct 1*

☐ _____   _____

☐ _____   _____

☐ _____   _____

☐ _____   _____

☐ _____   _____

☐ _____   _____

Action Items: **By**

Ask Robin if she wants to see a
movie with me on Thanksgiving
weekend.   *Oct 1*

_____   _____

_____   _____

_____   _____

_____   _____

_____   _____

_____   _____

_____   _____

_____   _____

_____   _____

_____   _____

_____   _____

_____   _____

_____   _____

Increasing Your Spirituality

There are many reasons why increasing our spirituality plays a part in a successful retirement, including:

- Our spiritual side helps us appreciate and enjoy the life we lead.
- Spirituality can provide comfort when we face difficult life events—events older adults are more likely to encounter.
- Spirituality often provides tools to deal with what life throws our way.
- Spirituality can also strengthen faith in ourselves and our abilities, helping us create the life we want in retirement.

It's worth emphasizing that there are many ways to increase our spiritual qualities. These are just a few:

- Attending services in a house of worship.
- Extending and giving help to others in need.
- Participating in activities such as drum circles.
- Seeking and accepting help in dealing with life's challenges.
- Taking time to reflect, meditate, or write in a journal.
- Being in nature by walking in the woods, going fishing, etc.
- Appreciating things in life as a way to acknowledge affirmations.
- Appreciating the joy and beauty of the simple things in life.

Spirituality in its many forms is an important part of a successful retirement. As you can see in the list above, we can tap into and strengthen our spirituality as we also work on other aspects of retirement. Take time to consider whether you are doing enough to feed your spirituality. If not, find suitable ways to do it and then take action.

Increasing Spirituality

Goals: **By**

☐ *Find a Torah study group.*   *Dec 15*
☐ _____   _____
☐ _____   _____
☐ _____   _____
☐ _____   _____
☐ _____   _____
☐ _____   _____

Action Items: **By**

Attend the synagogue for a few
     months.   *Start now*

_____   _____
_____   _____
_____   _____
_____   _____
_____   _____
_____   _____
_____   _____
_____   _____
_____   _____
_____   _____
_____   _____
_____   _____
_____   _____
_____   _____

Chapter 21

Applying Chapter 7
(Strategies for Success)

This chapter functions as a checklist for assessing and strengthening the strategies for a successful retirement. As I interviewed retirees, it became clear to me that those who applied similar strategies were able to generate their own success. The remaining chapters will help you do the same; however, there's no assumption that you don't currently apply such strategies to your life. Instead, I suggest using a threefold approach to working through the chapters on these strategies:

1. Review the relevant chapters in Part I.
2. Assess your strengths in each strategy as well as your current habits in applying them to planning, implementing, and maintaining a successful retirement.
3. Choose the strategies you want to strengthen and then follow through.

Here is a list of the strategies to use to manage your work and track your progress:

Assessed	Strengthen	Chapter/Strategy
☐	☐	Chapter 8 Imagine your legacy and use that to help guide your actions.
☐	☐	Chapter 9 Proactively work on enhancing relationships.
☐	☐	Chapter 10 Improve communication skills.
☐	☐	Chapter 11 Plan and stick to a budget.
☐	☐	Chapter 12 Organize papers and research services before needing them.
☐	☐	Chapter 13 Work with mentors (and consider being one yourself).

Chapter 22
Applying Chapter 8
(Imagine Your Legacy)

One trend I uncovered as I interviewed retirees is the tendency to think about how we will be remembered after we have passed on. Both successful and unsuccessful retirees commented on this. However, successful retirees applied the results of their introspection quite differently.

Unsuccessful retirees expressed a lot of regret—even bitterness—about their circumstances and the things they didn't do when they had the chance. Their focus was past-oriented, and their attitudes often amounted to a sense of victimhood. This isn't healthy, of course. One way to apply the success strategy of imagining your legacy is to consider how people might recall such attitudes once you have passed away. "She always wanted to go to the Louvre," someone might say. "Yes, it's sad she didn't go," another might reply, "but let's be honest; she preferred the drama of making it sound impossible."

Successful retirees use their personal idea of legacy to influence their lives in positive ways. They consider what is truly important and use it as a compass to guide their activities. For example, this could mean creating a viable plan for visiting Paris, or attending art exhibits featuring items on loan from the Louvre.

Successful retirees also use the consideration of legacy in its more traditional sense. Some arrange to leave monies, financial support, or items of value to people or organizations important to them. Others take a creative (and financially modest) approach. Examples include building a family tree and recording or writing a memoir. A retiree I recently met said he was slowly transferring thousands of slides into digital format. These slides include pictures of friends and their young families, so many beyond his own family will treasure this gift.

Our self-assessment of our potential legacy can also help us stop "sweating the small stuff" and embrace what psychologists often call our "authentic self." Such changes will affect our life in many positive ways in addition to informing how people will remember us. "I was so proud that she finally went to the Louvre," someone might say. "Yes, it's absolutely inspiring!" another might reply.

Imagine Your Legacy

Goals: By

☐ Find a way to support Ontario
  Parks.   2017
☐ _____   _____
☐ _____   _____
☐ _____   _____
☐ _____   _____
☐ _____   _____
☐ _____   _____

Action Items: By

Find upcoming events at local parks
  through Friends of Ontario Parks. End of 2016

_____   _____
_____   _____
_____   _____
_____   _____
_____   _____
_____   _____
_____   _____
_____   _____
_____   _____
_____   _____
_____   _____
_____   _____
_____   _____
_____   _____

Chapter 23
Applying Chapter 9 (Proactively Build and Enhance Relationships)

In retirement, people often find themselves isolated for the first time. Frankly, some find this pleasant—no more dealing with grouchy fellow commuters or demanding customers.

It's true that each of us needs different kinds of companionship in different amounts, but make no mistake: Retirement is when we most need companionship. This even goes for "loners." If you count yourself in that category, I recommend you put extra effort into applying this success strategy.

Many successful retirees report that they had to adopt new habits to ensure they fulfilled their need for companionship. This generally involved being more proactive in developing new relationships and improving existing relationships. It will be helpful and effective to approach your self-assessment and apply the strategy differently according to each type of relationship. For example:

- Co-workers and colleagues: Without the shared context and contact of work, you need to forge a new path. This might include letting go of some work relationships and taking steps to nurture others.

- Friends and acquaintances: This often includes

proactively putting yourself in places where you can meet potential new friends. On the other hand, enhancing relationships with current friends and acquaintances adds depth and breadth.

- Your partner: Retirement often affects this relationship the most, and so enhancing it has particular importance. Not mentioned in Part I is that many retirees without a partner apply this success strategy to add a most special companion to their life!

- Family members: Familial relationships are often extra beneficial—as well as extra challenging. It might be time to work on these relationships too.

Proactively Build and Enhance Relationships

Goals: ## By

☐ Identify colleagues I want to
   stay in touch with.   Feb 28

☐ _____   _____

☐ _____   _____

☐ _____   _____

☐ _____   _____

☐ _____   _____

☐ _____   _____

Action Items: ## By

Update profile on LinkedIn so
others can find me.   Feb 28

_____   _____

_____   _____

_____   _____

_____   _____

_____   _____

_____   _____

_____   _____

_____   _____

_____   _____

_____   _____

_____   _____

_____   _____

_____   _____

_____   _____

Chapter 24

Applying Chapter 10
(Improve Communication)

My interviews with retirees also revealed that improving communication skills is a key strategy for success. There are four reasons for this:

1. Even couples who have had excellent communication before retirement can experience difficulty when one or both of them retire. When you have less time apart, and less "space" to do your own thing and/or put things into perspective, past communication methods and habits might no longer work as well.

2. When one or both partners feel they've been misunderstood or marginalized in some way, spending more time together tends to exacerbate that strain on a relationship. Unresolved hurts and resentments come to the surface more readily or more often.

3. Retirement can be a time when family members and friends decide they know what's best for you. Improving your ability to communicate helps you use the good advice, soothe their concerns, and keep healthy boundaries at the same time.

4. A successful retirement includes personal growth, including developing new and stronger communication skills.

Strong communication skills help couples create and implement the shared aspects of a holistic retirement plan as well as be mutually supportive of individual goals and activities. Strong communication skills help individuals develop relationships with family and friends as well as work successfully with advisors and mentors. Use this chapter to assess your communication skills and determine any needed plan of action.

If you are part of a couple, copy the assessment, goals, and action items pages so each person has a set. Complete your assessments separately and then discuss the results. As noted in Part I, communication often improves even when only one person works on their individual skills. Don't let your partner's lack of participation hold you back.

Improve Communication

Goals: **By**

☐ *Share and discuss our*
  assessments.   *May 15*

☐ _____   _____

☐ _____   _____

☐ _____   _____

☐ _____   _____

☐ _____   _____

☐ _____   _____

Action Items: **By**

Decide if we will share and
discuss our assessments.   *May 1*

_____   _____

_____   _____

_____   _____

_____   _____

_____   _____

_____   _____

_____   _____

_____   _____

_____   _____

_____   _____

_____   _____

_____   _____

_____   _____

Self-Assessment: Improving Communication

Self-assessment involves asking yourself some questions. The questions below are worded to include a partner, but they certainly apply to anyone, including a friend who is very important to you, your adult children, and other family members.

As you complete the self-assessment, imagine conversations, whether lighthearted discussions or heated disagreements, with people important to you. Try to get a detailed image or many recollections in mind and then work through the questions.

Important: You'll be far more successful if you focus on yourself rather than your partner's or another person's bad habits or failings. Changing how *you* communicate often has an extremely positive affect on how others communicate with you.

1. Do I tune out when my partner says something I don't agree with or don't want to hear?

   _____
   _____
   _____

2. Do I often believe I know in advance what my partner is going to say?

   _____
   _____
   _____

3. Am I often forming a rebuttal or response in my head while my partner is talking?

_____

_____

_____

4. Do I accumulate little resentments until I feel very upset about them?

_____

_____

_____

5. Do I interrupt? Do I try to hurry things up by jumping in to say something?

_____

_____

_____

6. Do I acknowledge my partner's point of view, wants, needs, opinions, and feelings? If so, how?

_____

_____

_____

7. Do I often bring up important issues or topics when my partner is probably not in a mood to talk? If so, why do I do that?

_____

_____

_____

8. Do I sometimes correct my partner's grammar or word choice even when having an important or tense discussion?

_____

_____

_____

9. Do I talk with friends to process my thoughts and feelings or to vent, or do I talk with friends instead of talking with my partner? Which occurs most often?

_____

_____

_____

10. In terms of communication, I wish my partner wouldn't _____ because it makes me feel _____ .

_____

_____

_____

11. I know my partner is listening when....

_____

_____

_____

12. My partner shows me they value what I think or have to say by....

_____

_____

_____

13. Our communication strengths include....

_____

_____

_____

Do you have suggestions for additional self-assessment questions? Please share them with me so I can share them with others. Please contact me at ramgt@rogers.com.

Post-Assessment Considerations

The significance of communication was likely apparent as you read the self-assessment questions. Being human, you might even have fudged your responses a bit (or at least were tempted to). Either way, it's important to sort through the issues and clarify the things you wish to work on. The following tips, and those in Chapter 9, can help you improve your communication skills:

- *You tune out when the other person says something you don't agree with or don't want to hear.* The other person can usually tell you have tuned out or are only half-listening, and their interpretation of that almost always adds communication challenges. For example, your lack of attention can send the message that you don't value the person's thoughts, opinions, and feelings. To avoid this, practice active listening to ensure you stay engaged, and express your own thoughts, including disagreement, when the time comes.

  Lack of attention can also signal that you intend to act on your own wishes regardless of the other person's wishes. To avoid this, again, practice active listening, including repeating their concerns back to them to find out if you're hearing them correctly. Try to come to an agreement on what you will or will not do.

  If you tune out because you're fearful of what's being said, your inattention can still send the same messages. This can escalate into a power struggle, even though at least one person is acting out of fear. Take a deep breath, and express yourself. If you find that you too often have great difficulty in doing so, it might be appropriate to work with a counsellor or therapist.

- *You believe you know what the other person will say before they say it.* Some people believe they know what the other person's response will be and therefore don't raise certain issues at all. This isn't a healthy approach. Although raising such issues is bound to feel uncomfortable at first, practice will make it easier. Work with a counsellor if needed.

  Believing you know a person's response in advance can also lead to wording things in ways you hope will generate a certain outcome. This isn't necessarily a negative or unproductive method of communication; however, like most things, it can go too far. Avoid trying to "make" the other person feel a certain way. Beware of condescension as well.

- *You form a response or rebuttal while the other person is speaking.* This is appropriate for formal debate and legal proceedings but is otherwise counterproductive because you're not paying full attention to the other person. In other words, you're essentially tuning out! Forming a response while others are speaking also makes you more prone to interrupting them—another counterproductive habit.

  If this is a communication habit you wish to address, begin by considering why you do it. Do you think you already know what the other person will say? Is your sense of disagreement, or fear, prompting you to tune out? If so, apply the tips listed above.

Some of us begin formulating our response in advance because we need enough time to do it well. If this is the case, give yourself time after the person has finished speaking. Say, "I need to gather my thoughts a bit," and then do that. If you need more time, including to calm down if you're feeling upset, then ask for it: "I'd like to take a while to think about what you've shared. Is that okay?" Making this a request avoids behaving in ways that the other person might interpret as you ignoring them or shutting them out.

- *You accumulate resentments until you feel very upset.* Even tiny resentments can have a powerful effect if they accumulate, and when you finally express your feelings, they're out of proportion, making it quite difficult for the other person to understand why you're so upset. That, in turn, makes it hard to know how to respond. Potential solutions include the following:

  1. Prevention: Bring things up as they occur rather than letting them fester.

  2. Lighten up: Does it really matter if a wet towel was left on the floor or if the hall light was left on?

  3. Renegotiate agreements: If someone thinks they do too many chores, they might feel unappreciated for the things they do, etc. See if you can address these little issues before they snowball.

  4. Ask for appreciation when you need it: One couple

I know uses a team-building technique taught by Playfair. One of them will *ask* for a standing ovation—and gets it! (See www.playfair.com for more information.)

- *You suspect that maybe you, on very rare occasions, slightly "interrupt" others.* I've used a bit of humour here because we sometimes don't realize how often we interrupt others. One surefire way to find out is to ask your family and close friends about it. More subtle signs of interruptions include giving annoyed looks or exasperated sighs after we've asked a question or shared an observation or opinion—we sometimes do this when the other person hasn't finished speaking.

  One of the reasons we interrupt people is because we're afraid we will forget our question or point. Make an effort to hold back until the other person is done speaking. You might at first forget your question or lose your train of thought, but with practice you will be able to hold on to them.

  People who live alone or converse infrequently can lose their ability to sense when others have finished speaking. If you suspect that this has created an interruption habit in you, practice silently counting to five after you *think* a person has paused.

- *Acknowledging the other person's point of view, wants, needs, opinions, and feelings.* Ways to acknowledge these things include nodding, repeating back what we think we heard, and making affirming statements. Note that these are all actions. If you were unable to answer this question by describing actions, this is an area you need to work on.

- *You tend to bring up important issues or topics when you know the other person isn't in a mood to talk.* The following are some of the common reasons behind this poor communication habit:

  1. You think the other person "never" wants to talk. In this case, ask the person to name a time when they're willing to talk. Try to avoid using a resentful tone as you do so.

  2. You think or believe their response will be negative—why not just get it over with? This is self-sabotage. Force yourself to wait for a better time and/or ask the person when they'll be willing to talk.

  3. Your natural communication times don't often coincide (e.g., one of you is a morning person and the other is a night owl). If this is the case, agree to talk when your times overlap, or make an effort to talk at a time of their preference instead of yours.

- *You have a habit of correcting the other person's grammar or word choice.* This is highly condescending and dismissive. It's also a way to deflect from the real topic. Never do this when you're having an important, tense, or fraught discussion, even if your loved one is comfortable with the practice at other times. You might need to halt the practice altogether to avoid applying it at the wrong time.

- *You talk with friends to avoid talking with your partner or other loved one.* Many people clarify their thoughts and feelings by talking things through with trusted friends. However, take care not to do these things in place of meaningful communication with your loved one.

  Venting can also be quite helpful. On the other hand, continual or repeated griping can exacerbate what you might otherwise let go. Consider whether the activity is adjusting your attitudes in negative ways or if you are truly letting off steam in a healthy manner.

- *You wish the other person wouldn't do certain things.* Does your partner or other loved one do something that pushes your buttons? If you choose to share the answer to this self-assessment question with your loved one, prepare one or two suggestions for what they could do instead and share those too. You might find suitable suggestions in the answers you gave to the remaining self-assessment questions.

  Remember, too, that you can work on your response to things that push your buttons. In other words, you can defuse these buttons yourself. This includes considering the possibility that your response is driven more by old "baggage" than it is by your loved one.

- *You know the other person is listening and they show you they value what you think or say when they do certain things.* You can use the answers to these questions to tell your loved one what you appreciate about them. Being specific helps people know what to repeat as well. The answers can also help you understand how to better show your loved one you too are listening and value what they have to say. Emulating their actions can speak the loudest.

- *You know the communication strengths between you and the other person.* Were you able to identify at least one communication strength between you and your loved one? Good! Recognizing current strengths will inspire you to work on adding to the list.

Communication is a two-way street, but taking steps to improve your own skills can make a tremendous difference. Focus on making desired changes on your end. Be patient—both with yourself and with the amount of time it takes for things to change.

Seek assistance in improving communication skills as appropriate. Consider reading self-help books, attending lectures on the subject, and asking friends how they handle certain communication issues. Of course, there are also many professionals who can help in this area.

Be sure to re-evaluate and revisit your progress, successes, and strengths often!

Chapter 25

Applying Chapter 11
(Plan and Stick to a Budget)

As noted in Part I, budgeting is something of a lost art. Many of us fall out of the habit as we become more financially secure; it's an outcome of no longer needing to watch every penny. Others were never introduced to budgeting, which is an unfortunate side effect of reluctance to discuss financial issues even among family (or especially among family).

Whether you've never budgeted or you came to the point where you felt it was no longer needed, whether you're preparing to retire or are currently retired, now is the time to apply budgeting as a strategy for retirement success.

The budgeting process is described in overview in Chapter 11. This chapter here in Part II includes worksheets you can use to establish a budget, which you can then review and add certain points as you complete the work.

Online Resources and Software Tools
Type "creating a personal budget" into a search engine, and you'll find many articles and tips. Although search results will certainly change over time, when I did this myself, the results included instructions for setting up a Microsoft Excel spreadsheet for budgeting. This is a program many of us already own.

There are also software programs designed for budgeting and related financial management tasks. If you shop for these, be sure to choose a program specifically designed for personal use (not small business). A prime example includes Quicken Cash Manager, but be aware that this program doesn't include features for monitoring your investments. If you want those features, you'll need to opt for Quicken Home & Business. Visit quicken.intuit.ca for more information.

More recently, online options for budgeting have hit the market. One that has received a lot of buzz is Mint, which is now available in Canada. Visit www.mint.com/canada for more information.

Regardless of which option you choose, be sure to do some research beforehand. Ask your friends and family what they use. Read reviews and read about the features of each product (including security and privacy features). If you still have any doubts, ask your financial advisor for feedback.

A Consideration for Couples

If only one of you has been managing the finances and bills on a daily basis, change that system so both of you are fully aware, involved, and equipped to handle it on your own if necessary.

Create a Budget

The first set of goals applies overall. The second set of goals might be an outcome of the budgeting process.

Goals: **By**

☐ Calculate current expenses and
   income.   _____

☐ Consult with advisor to determine
   if expenses should be reduced.   _____

☐ Create and implement any needed
   plan of action.   _____

☐ Create or find tools and implement
   plan for managing budget on an
   ongoing basis.   _____

☐ Couples: Create and implement
   plan for sharing budgeting
   and bill-paying tasks.   _____

☐ _____   _____

☐ _____   _____

Additional Goals: **By**

☐ *Reduce housing expense by $275.*   *Jan* 31

☐ _____   _____

☐ _____   _____

☐ _____   _____

☐ _____   _____

Create a Budget (cont'd)

Action Items: **By**

Create a cheat sheet for charitable
donations so we don't go over total
budget. Sign up for online banking.   *Dec 1*

_____   _____

_____   _____

_____   _____

_____   _____

_____   _____

_____   _____

_____   _____

_____   _____

_____   _____

_____   _____

_____   _____

_____   _____

_____   _____

_____   _____

_____   _____

_____   _____

_____   _____

_____   _____

_____   _____

_____   _____

Tips for Using the Budgeting Worksheets

The overall budgeting process is shown below with tips for using the worksheets provided.

1. *Calculate your current or projected monthly expenses.* There are two blank monthly expenses worksheets. (Make copies before you begin.) Use the first worksheet to calculate your current or projected expenses. Use the second worksheet to show your budget—the amount you intend to spend. This is where you'll show any changes (e.g., you've decided to spend less on groceries).

2. *Calculate your current or projected income.* There are two blank income worksheets. (Make copies in case you need more.) These are for making notes as you and your advisors examine various what-if scenarios as needed (e.g., what if you work part-time or retire at a later date).

3. *Add savings for expected and unexpected expenses.* This step is specified because before retirement we tend to handle expenses such as replacing a car or roof as they arise. Successful retirees report that they think much further ahead in retirement. There is a line provided on the budget worksheet for you to do the same.

4. *Compare your income to your expenses and make changes as appropriate.* This is a vital step that goes far beyond simple math. For example, the expense amount cannot simply be divided into the amounts you

have in your TFSA or IRA, your RRSP or 401K, your TSAs, etc. Even if those funds are in savings as opposed to stocks that change in value, the tax implications are extremely complex. You will almost certainly need assistance to make good choices.

Successful retirees work with professionals to determine if they're on a sound path or if they need to make changes such as reducing housing expense (the most common major change). Seek out qualified advisors to work with. Use the worksheets provided here, as well as the worksheet detailing housing expense, to inform the above process. (A worksheet for notes and questions is also provided so you can write things down before you speak to your advisors.)

Current Monthly Expenses

Total housing expense
     (from Chapter 19 worksheet) $_____

Groceries $_____

Restaurants, casual takeout, etc. $_____

Movies and other entertainment $_____

Dry cleaning, laundry, shoe shine or
     repair, etc. $_____

TV service $_____

Internet $_____

All telephones (detail elsewhere) $_____

Gym membership, classes, green
     fees, etc. (detail elsewhere) $_____

Hobby costs $_____

Automobile, boat, other vehicle loans $_____

Automobile, boat, other vehicle
     maintenance $_____

Automobile, boat, other vehicle
     insurance $_____

Volunteering and socializing
     expenses $_____

Misc. purchases $_____

Credit cards and personal loans
     total (detail elsewhere) $_____

Health and dental insurance $_____

Savings (for travel, large purchase,
    gifts, etc.) $_____

Support (children, grandchildren,
    ex-partners, etc.) $_____

Pet expenses $_____

Charitable contributions $_____

Other: $_____

Other: $_____

Other: $_____

Other: $_____

Other: $_____

Total $_____

Monthly Expenses Budget

Total housing expense

    (see Chapter 19 worksheet) $_____

Groceries $_____

Restaurants, casual takeout, etc. $_____

Movies and other entertainment $_____

Dry cleaning, laundry, shoe shine or

    repair, etc. $_____

TV service $_____

Internet $_____

All telephones (detail elsewhere) $_____

Gym membership, classes, green

    fees, etc. (detail elsewhere) $_____

Hobby costs $_____

Automobile, boat, other vehicle loans $_____

Automobile, boat, other vehicle

    maintenance $_____

Automobile, boat, other vehicle

    insurance $_____

Volunteering and socializing

    expenses $_____

Misc. purchases $_____

Credit cards and personal loans

    total (detail elsewhere) $_____

Health and dental insurance $_____

Savings (for travel, large purchase,
    gifts, etc.) $_____

Support (children, grandchildren,
    ex-partners, etc.) $_____

Pet expenses $_____

Charitable contributions $_____

(Added) Savings for expected and
    unexpected expenses $_____

Other: $_____

Other: $_____

Other: $_____

Other: $_____

Other: $_____

Total $_____

Monthly Income

Canada Pension Plan/Social Security	$_____
Annuities	$_____
Pensions	$_____
Retirement plans (including RRIFs or IRAs)	$_____
Income from property	$_____
Other income:	$_____
Other income:	$_____
Other income:	$_____
Total	$_____

Canada Pension Plan/Social Security	$_____
Annuities	$_____
Pensions	$_____
Retirement plans (including RRIFs or IRAs)	$_____
Income from property	$_____
Other income:	$_____
Other income:	$_____
Other income:	$_____
Total	$_____

Budgeting Notes / Questions for Advisor(s)

_____
_____
_____
_____
_____
_____
_____
_____
_____
_____
_____
_____
_____
_____
_____
_____
_____
_____
_____
_____
_____
_____
_____
_____
_____
_____

Chapter 26
Applying Chapter 12
(Organize Papers and Research Services Before Needing Them)

Most of us have a home office of some kind. Some of us have an entire room, complete with desk, computer, filing cabinet, and bookcases. Some of us have a corner of the kitchen table and several boxes of records stored in the garage or under the bed.

Whatever the type of home office you happen to have, take a moment to picture it. Now imagine that you have suddenly fallen seriously ill. Your partner has spent hours by your side in the hospital and is exhausted. However, she knows bills must be paid and heads home to do that. It's been several months since she handled this household chore. The pile of bills is easy to find. The computer boots right up. She types in the URL…and draws a blank on the password. After three incorrect attempts, the system locks her out. The help desk is closed until Monday. Your partner's burden just got a bit heavier.

The above scenario is quite common but easily prevented. The completion of this organization project will prevent it from happening. The goal is to create references others can use to take care of certain daily tasks as well as the sombre tasks associated with someone's passing.

Let us return to the image of you in the hospital, this

time imagining you're well enough to return home for rehabilitation. Unless you're already had this experience, you might believe that hospital staff would handle the details of such a transition (e.g., patient and family member interviews, discharge planning, caregiver education, etc.). This is not often the case. Completion of this research project will prepare you to better handle the situation (as well as inform other life decisions).

Anyone who assists when you or your family are in need will be able to use the resulting references. After all, it could be a child, a neighbour, or a friend doing their best to help—someone who has no idea which pile of bills is the unpaid pile.

The goals on the following worksheet include evaluating the need for a will, a living trust, and powers of attorney for convenience. Consult with advisors to determine their need and usefulness and then add goals as appropriate.

A list of things you might wish to include among your references is provided following the action items worksheet. Remember to distribute this and other documents to those who might need to use them (e.g., executor, children, first and second person given powers of attorney, etc.).

Organize Papers and Research Services

Goals: By

☐ Evaluate the need for a will, a
  living trust, and powers of
  attorney.   _____

Note any follow-up goals below, including distribution:

☐ _____   _____

☐ _____   _____

☐ _____   _____

These goals apply to the reference document described in
Part I:

☐ Create a reference document.   _____

☐ Provide copies of the reference
  document to those who might
  need to use it.   _____

☐ _____   _____

☐ _____   _____

☐ _____   _____

Research project goals:

☐ Complete research project.   _____

☐ Create an additional reference
  document or add information
  to the above reference document. _____

☐ _____   _____

Organize Papers and Research Services (cont'd)

Action Items: **By**

Get powers of attorney form for
    primary bank account.   Aug 18

_____   _____

_____   _____

_____   _____

_____   _____

_____   _____

_____   _____

_____   _____

_____   _____

_____   _____

_____   _____

_____   _____

_____   _____

_____   _____

_____   _____

_____   _____

_____   _____

_____   _____

_____   _____

_____   _____

_____   _____

_____   _____

_____   _____

What to Include in the Reference Document

The checklist provided here will help you create a thorough reference document. See Chapter 12 for information on why to include the following items.

☐ People to be notified at the time of your death. Includes attorney, executor, trustee, accountant, financial advisor. Show name, role (e.g., attorney), and phone number.

☐ Friends and relatives you wish to be notified of your death as soon as possible. Show name, address, and phone number. Also indicate where someone can find names and contact information for others who will wish to know (e.g., "See red address book in desk drawer.")

☐ Prepaid funeral, cremation, or mortuary arrangements. Include contact information and any relevant details (e.g., "Prepaid for simple casket.")

☐ Location of important personal papers, including birth and marriage certificates, military papers, deeds, certificates of insurance, current and old mortgage documents, and diplomas (if they're important to you).

☐ All insurance policies: life, health, auto, homeowners, etc. Include contact information.

☐ Exact location of any safe deposit boxes and their keys. Show institution name and address of where the boxes are located.

☐ Bank and credit union accounts and locations. Show institution name, account numbers and type, address, and phone number. If you have certain service providers, show their names and numbers as well.

- [ ] Primary accounts used to pay bills. Provide related on-line banking user name and password (but you might wish to do this separately).
- [ ] Monthly household expenses and bills. Note any that use automatic debit and should be cancelled immediately (e.g., health club dues).
- [ ] Income sources, including CPP/QPP or Social Security, annuities, TFSA or IRA, etc. Show current monthly amounts. Be sure your partner knows how income will change when you pass away.
- [ ] Any account beneficiaries other than your partner. Show account numbers and list beneficiary names and their current contact information. (However, the financial institution will contact beneficiaries and handle any distribution.)
- [ ] User names and passwords of your email accounts.
- [ ] Credit cards with issuer name and service phone number. Indicate which you usually carry with you.
- [ ] Vehicles, if you own more than one. List the location of any boats, RVs, etc.
- [ ] Clubs or memberships, including country club, hunting club, social clubs, etc. Show contact information and any dues.
- [ ] Indicate where past income, property, and business tax information is stored. Include tax preparer's or advisor's contact information.
- [ ] Investments and investment accounts. Include the location of statements.
- [ ] Key valuables and their locations. Include wishes for gifting these as appropriate.
- [ ] Any trusts other than your living trust as well as any

loans you've made. Include the contact information of trustees and borrowers as well as where to find the documents.

☐ Local assisted living residences, short-term skilled nursing facilities, and in-home care providers. Show type and contact information and any preferences.

☐ Any household dos and don'ts, such as general tips or wishes for caring for pets.

☐ _____

☐ _____

☐ _____

☐ _____

☐ _____

Do you have suggestions of items to add to these references? Please share by emailing me (ramgt@rogers.com).

Research Project

Experience is a great but often difficult teacher. The overall purpose of this project is to spare you and your loved ones from learning certain things the hard way. As noted in Part I, the likelihood of needing these things might seem—and be—far off. Nonetheless, I encourage you to complete this research now and include the information in your reference document.

☐ Residential options: Contact several assisted living residences in your area and/or areas to which you might relocate. Also consider visiting at least some of them in person.

• Are the options many or limited?

- What kind of care is provided?
- What costs are involved?
- Does insurance help meet the costs?
- What about options for transitioning from independent to assisted care?
- What is the process to get in?
- Are short-term stays permitted?

☐ Care in your home: Contact several reputable care providers.
- What are the rates (including for handling medications, monitoring blood pressure, etc.)?
- What kinds of housekeeping, meal preparation, errands, and driving will they do?

☐ Ask friends about independent caregivers to get a sense of cost as well as the pros and cons.

☐ Other assistance: Consider additional service providers.
- Explore the cost and availability for help with errands, transportation to and from medical and other appointments, light housekeeping, and/or meal preparation.
- Does the local phone company and/or utility offer special services?
- What is your local elder assistance or resource organization?

☐ Learn about the safety net, especially for residential long-term care.

- Canadian citizens: What are the eligibility requirements of the programs for your province or area to which you might relocate? What special programs are available, and how might budget issues affect them?
- U.S. citizens: What are the eligibility requirements of the Medicare program for your state or states to which you might relocate? What special programs are available, and how might budget issues affect them?

Chapter 27

Applying Chapter 13 (Work with Mentors)

As you might imagine, this success strategy is particularly near and dear to me. I, of course, hope to be something of a mentor to you, just as the thousands of retirees I've interviewed have helped me with my own success. However, these "virtual" mentors have the best effect when you also have personal mentors.

If you are part of a couple, each person should work through the process of considering a mentor individually. (Copy the worksheets below so each person has a set.) Compare notes to help determine your next steps. You might decide to each get your own private mentor. There's nothing wrong with that, but don't let it replace the work you should do as a couple.

What Kind of Help Does a Mentor Provide?

In Chapter 13, I described the first step in finding a mentor as acknowledging that you probably need help to have a great retirement. Now take that further by outlining the input and guidance you're open to receiving as well as the kind you don't want. Here are some things to consider:

- Do you want a devil's advocate, an avid cheerleader, or both?

- Do you want help creating your retirement vision? Do you want someone to critique it once it's drafted? Neither? Both?

- Are there parts of your vision you want help with and parts that are off limits? If some are off limits, which parts are they?

- Do you want to reserve certain parts of your retirement plan for existing mentors? For example, will your financial advisor and/or accountant work with you on budgeting?

- Are there parts of your retirement plan you intend to work on as a priority, or skip, no matter what a mentor might say?

The Help I Seek from a Mentor

It's okay to begin with what you don't want—many people think of that first. Afterward, consider its opposite to see if you can also identify at least some of what you do want.

_____

_____

_____

_____

_____

_____

_____

_____

_____

_____

_____

_____

_____

_____

_____

_____

_____

_____

_____

_____

_____

_____

_____

_____

_____

Who Fits the Bill?

This step is to consider who in your social circle or family belongs on your short list. This is not to say there *is* someone or that they will necessarily agree to be your mentor, but it's an important early step for finding candidates. As you run through your mental list, consider the following:

- Are you looking for someone who has already "been there, done that"?
- Do you expect them to share details of what was behind their choices and information about the things they learned the hard way?
- Do you instead prefer someone who is creating and implementing their retirement vision at roughly the same time as you?

If some people do indeed come to mind as potential mentors, clarify the following points for yourself (you might want to share your thoughts with them later):

- Why would this person be a good mentor?
- What is it about them you respect and appreciate?

If there were instances in the past in which the potential mentors have assisted you, add these points for consideration:

- Did you have clashes as part of the process? Were they beneficial, acceptable, or something to avoid next time?
- Did you feel genuine appreciation and were you able to fully express it?

If No Potential Mentors Come to Mind

Remember that your financial advisor might already be an important mentor. Also, many senior centres offer peer counselling and coaching. You might find good candidates among them.

Consider finding a partner or starting a group focused on planning and implementing a successful retirement. (You might wish to work through the senior centre or ask your financial advisor to help you with this.)

Finally, consider engaging a professional life coach.

Potential Mentors

Many people have more than one mentor. Couples often find that one partner fills a mentor role because of their expertise. If you see your partner that way, include them on the list!

Are there few or no potential mentors who come to mind? Use this space to note ideas of where to find one. (Remember to add this to the action items below as well.)

_____

_____

_____

_____

_____

_____

_____

_____

_____

_____

_____

_____

_____

_____

_____

_____

_____

_____

_____

_____

_____

Establish a Relationship with Your Mentors
This step includes approaching potential mentors to discuss a mentor relationship. Be mindful that you are making a request—one they should feel free to turn down.

When approaching a paid professional, such as a life coach, consider the following:

- It's advisable to talk with more than one before choosing.

- Explore the potential fit by talking about the kind of help you seek. (As indicated above.)

- Discuss time commitments. Ask about any long-term contract requirements and any requirements for advance payment.

- Look for professionals who offer a free or discounted initial meeting.

When approaching friends or family members, consider the following:

- It might be best to begin with *why* you think they'd be a good mentor. What is it about them you appreciate and respect?

- Talk about the kinds of help and support you seek (and what you're not looking for). Ask for their thoughts on any additions to that. After all, that's part of why you seek a mentor.

- Discuss any concerns either of you have. This includes talking about any areas of conflict or potential conflict.

- Cover specifics including how often you'd meet, where you'd meet, and whether you both want a long-term time commitment.

- Discuss the above and then give both of you time to think things over.

When creating and using a work group, consider the following:

- Talk about how the group will work together and how often you'll meet.

- Discuss whether the group will use individual and/or group "assignments."

- Discuss whether group members can request accountability measures or if they're required.

- Have one person act as facilitator in each meeting, and rotate the role among all members. This person manages time and reminds people about the group's working guidelines.

Engage Mentors

Goals:	By
☐ Complete consideration of engaging mentors.	_____
☐ Begin seeking at least one mentor.	_____
☐ If possible, begin working with a mentor.	_____
☐ _____	_____

Action Items:	By
See if Suzanne and Lois want to begin a group.	Jan 15
_____	_____
_____	_____
_____	_____
_____	_____
_____	_____
_____	_____
_____	_____
_____	_____
_____	_____
_____	_____
_____	_____
_____	_____
_____	_____
_____	_____

Appendix A
Financial Planning —
How Much Will I Need?

How much money do you need to retire comfortably? Is it $250,000? $500,000? $1 million or more? What is a realistic amount based on your current and visualized lifestyle? Most people feel they need more money than they have. Ask a person with $500,000 in retirement savings how much they need for retirement, and they will likely say, "More than what I currently have." Ask a person with $1 million or $3 million in retirement savings, and the answer will be the same.

The trick to a happy retirement financially speaking is not to concentrate on amassing an abnormal amount of wealth but to determine how much money will make you feel secure. In other words, how much money will you need to live and fulfill your visualized retirement lifestyle?

In a practical sense, how you spend your retirement time will determine how much money you'll need. If you plan to travel the world or indulge in expensive hobbies such as luxury sailing, then your financial needs will be much greater than someone with more modest plans. What you don't want is to envision a retirement you realistically cannot afford. All this does is cause anxiety and unease. By creating a retirement that is realistic and affordable, you gain satisfaction and peace of mind. Calculating a good estimate of the cost of your retirement plans is the key to determining the amount of money you'll need to save.

Part 1: Estimating Retirement Lifestyle Cost

Ask yourself the following questions:

1. At what age do my partner and I want to retire?

   Me _____ My partner _____

2. Do we plan to downsize our home?
   Yes   No

3. Will we move out of the city to a less expensive home in the country?
   Yes   No

4. Will we move to a retirement community?
   Yes   No

5. Do we want to rent or own a vacation home?
   Yes   No

6. Will we spend time in warmer climates each year?
   Yes   No
   If so, for how long?

   _____
   _____
   _____

7. Do we plan to travel abroad?

      Yes   No

   How often and how far?

_____

_____

_____

8. Will we stay in upscale hotels?

      Yes   No

9. Do we plan to make any major purchases or renovations?   Yes   No

10. Will I (we) work part-time while retired?

      Yes   No

11. Will I (we) help support any family members?

      Yes   No

12. What hobbies will my partner and I pursue? What will they cost?

Hobby	Cost
_____	_____
_____	_____
_____	_____
_____	_____
_____	_____
_____	_____
_____	_____
_____	_____

13. Do we plan to frequently dine out, attend the theatre, and go to the movies?

     Yes   No

14. Do we plan to spend all our capital during our lifetime or do we plan to leave an estate?

     Spend it all   Leave an estate

By answering the above questions, you will start to get a sense of how much money you will need in retirement. Obviously, there is no single amount that will guarantee an adequate retirement, but most financial advisors in North America use a guideline of 60 to 80 percent of what you earned in the years right before retirement to determine the amount you will need to maintain your standard of living in retirement. This assumes that you will live mortgage- and rent-free and that you will be able to live somewhat more inexpensively in retirement. The closer you are to the 80 percent mark when you retire, the more comfortable you will likely be.

Part 2: Government Benefits

As part of your financial plan, take a close look at what you might receive from government pensions. Feel free to call the numbers below for more information or if you have any questions. Government pensions are indexed for inflation. This means they rise each year to cover the cost of inflation, and they are guaranteed for as long as you live.

1. Canada Pension Plan/Quebec Pension Plan (CPP/QPP)—Canada

For 2016, the maximum CPP/QPP retirement benefit for new recipients age sixty-five is $1,092.50 per month. You should determine how much you might receive from CPP/QPP from ages sixty through sixty-five and determine whether it makes economic sense to collect your CPP/QPP before age sixty-five. Your financial advisor or accountant will be able to assist with your answer.

I recommend you submit your application for CPP/QPP as early as twelve months before the month in which you want your pension to begin. To qualify for the monthly CPP/QPP pension, you must meet one of the following criteria:

1. You are sixty-five years of age or older.
2. You are between sixty and sixty-five years of age and have stopped working or have earnings from work below the maximum CPP/QPP retirement pension for two consecutive months.

If you elect to receive your pension at age sixty, your monthly payment will be 36 percent less than if you had taken it at sixty-five. If you take your pension after sixty-five, your monthly amount may be larger, by up to 42 percent at age seventy.

For information on CPP, call:
In Canada or the U.S.:
1-800-277-9914 (English)
1-800-277-9915 (French)
or visit www.esdc.gc.ca/en/cpp/

For information on QPP, call:
In Canada or the U.S.:
1-800-463-5185
or visit www.rrq.gouv.qc.ca/en/programmes/regime_rentes/

2. Old Age Security (OAS)—Canada

OAS is a basic benefit paid to all Canadians who are sixty-five and older and meet certain Canadian residency requirements. The maximum monthly payment amount from January to March 2016 was $570.52. Depending on other income, you might have to give some or all of OAS back.

To apply for OAS, you can submit your application up to twelve months before you turn sixty-five. If you are already sixty-five or older, send in your application as soon as possible so you won't lose any more payments.

For information on OAS, call:
In Canada or the U.S.:
1-800-277-9914 (English)
1-800-277-9915 (French)
or visit www.esdc.gc.ca/en/cpp/oas/index.page

3. Social Security—U.S.

The average American receives a portion of retirement income from Social Security. To qualify for Social Security retirement benefits, you need a certain number of credits. If you were born in 1929 or later, you need forty credits, which represents ten years of work. Your benefit payment amount is based on how much you earned during your working career. Higher lifetime earnings result in higher benefits.

In 2016, the maximum benefit at full retirement age is $2,787.80 per month. Full retirement age is between age sixty-six and sixty-seven, depending on your date of birth. However, your benefit payment is affected if you retire at a different age. If you retire at age sixty-two, the earliest possible retirement age for Social Security, the maximum benefit in 2016 is $2,102. If you retire at age seventy, the maximum benefit in 2016 is $3,576.

Supplemental Security Income (SSI)

SSI is a income supplement program available through Social Security. It is designed to help disabled adults and children with little or no income. It provides benefit payments to meet basic needs for food, clothing, and shelter.

For more information on Social Security, call:
1-800-772-1213
or visit www.socialsecurity.gov

Part 3: Company Pension Plans and Benefits
Now it's time to review your company pension plan and benefits. Company plans are as varied as the companies that offer them. Become familiar with your company's plan. See what it offers and how it can add to your other retirement income sources.

At the same time, ask about the continuance of your company life insurance, medical, health, and dental benefits when you retire.

Finally, if you have worked in another country (e.g., the U.K.), check with that country's pension authorities to determine your eligibility for a government pension.

Part 4: Savings Plans, Retirement Accounts, and Other Assets

Determine what you have in savings, your RRSPs or 401(k), and locked-in retirement accounts (LIRAs). List all income from non-registered investments as well. Be sure to look at interest from personal savings accounts and interest, dividends, and/or redemptions from GICs, mutual funds, stocks, and bonds. Don't forget the conversion of home equity, income from business assets and real estate, and the liquidation of personal assets.

Once you've listed all these assets, calculate your net worth using the net worth statement form below. Your net worth is the difference between what you own (assets) and what you owe (liabilities). It gives you a snapshot of your financial health at a specific point in time. Completing a net worth statement annually will help you assess your progress toward achieving your financial goals.

Appendix B
Finding and Using a Financial Advisor

If you don't have a financial advisor, find one. Choosing a financial advisor is a bit like committing to a marriage. You want to get it right because divorce is painful. Seek recommendations from your friends, your banker, your accountant, your insurance agent, and any other people you trust and respect. Be sure to check the credentials and references of potential financial advisors. Confirm their educational background and professional affiliations. Ask yourself, "Am I comfortable with this person, and can I trust them with my money?"

Here are some tips for selecting an advisor who is right for you:

1. Answer the following questions:
   - What's your level of financial understanding?
   - Do you have the time and interest to learn about investing?
   - Do you want to monitor your own investments on an ongoing basis, reach decisions to buy or sell investments, and then act on your decisions?

If you are a disciplined, financially educated person who will spend the necessary time, then being your own financial advisor is an option.

2. Write down what you expect an advisor to do for you, including the following:
    - Provide a written overall investment strategy that includes projected rates of returns and meets your needs and objectives.
    - Provide specific recommendations (purchase/sale) consistent with your investment strategy.
    - Answer all questions about investing and provide ongoing financial education.
    - Provide advice on tax implications.
    - Provide referrals to other professionals (i.e., insurance agent, tax accountant, retirement coach, etc.) where appropriate.
    - Be easily accessible by telephone and e-mail.
    - Call monthly with an update.
    - Meet quarterly to review investments.
    - Contact promptly if current events have a major impact on investments.
    - Conduct purchases and sales in a timely manner at the best available prices.
    - Provide clear, understandable, and complete written statements of investments and return rates.
    - Disclose all costs, commissions, and fees.

3. Make a list of questions for a potential financial advisor, including the following:
    - What are your qualifications and experience?
    - How long has your firm been in business?
    - Does your firm sell investments as well as provide advice?
    - What is your investment philosophy?

- Do you personally buy and sell financial products? If so, what products are you qualified to sell and what products do you typically recommend?
- Do you prepare individual investment plans based on each client's personal situation?
- How often will we talk and/or meet? Where will the meetings be held?
- How quickly will you respond if I call or email you?
- How are you paid? What fees does your firm charge for account administration?
- What research, newsletters, etc., do you and your firm provide to clients?
- What kind of account statements do you provide and how frequently?
- How will I know the performance of my investments?
- Do you provide statements with the original cost, current market value, and return rate of each investment?
- What is your firm's procedure for handling client complaints?

4. Develop a list of potential advisors. Here are some ways to identify candidates:
   - Canvass your family, friends, and business associates for names of advisors they recommend and why.
   - Consult the "find an advisor" section of the website of professional financial advisor organizations.
   - Scan the financial media (business sections of

newspapers, websites, magazines) for articles referencing or written by financial advisors.
- Attend a financial forum or seminars presented by investment advisors of brokerage firms.

5. Sift through the leads you have collected and make a short list of two or three advisors.

6. Interview all the advisors on your short list. Ask each candidate the same questions and take notes on how each one answers,

7. Take some time to reflect on the interviews.

8. Perform your due diligence. Confirm that the chosen advisor and their firm have the qualifications and provide the services they indicated. Check with the appropriate governing body that the advisor and firm are listed as members in good standing (qualifications, adherence to the code of business conduct, complaints on file if any, etc.).

9. Contact the chosen advisor, indicate your interest, and arrange a meeting. Request the advisor provide a written agreement covering:
- Your level of risk tolerance
- Your desired target asset allocation, including the allowable range and process for maintaining the allocation
- The range of expected return rates of your portfolio

- Any investment restrictions
- All fees and charges
- The frequency and nature of contact with the advisor
- The reporting on the performance of your investments, including the benchmarks used for comparison

10. After six months with your new advisor, review their performance and decide if they have met your expectations. If not, consider hiring the advisor who came second in your original search. If you're not satisfied, don't hesitate to change advisors. The new advisor should take care of the paperwork required to transfer your account.

When it comes to investing, no one has all the answers. No one can predict what financial markets will do beyond educated guesses. However, between you, your partner, and your financial advisor, you increase the odds of making good financial decisions. Three heads are better than one!

Below is an example of a couple facing important financial decisions:

Ron and Charlotte began making contributions to their RRSPs in their early forties. Until that time, their money was spent on mortgage payments, providing for themselves and their three children, paying off school debts, and paying for other living expenses. When they began seriously contributing to their retirement fund, they were afraid there would not be enough money for them to travel once a year to an exotic location, attend concerts, pay for Ron's golfing and Charlotte's photography hobby, help out their grandchildren with school, and enjoy life in general. Ron and Charlotte believed the hype at the time that stated they would need over $1 million in savings to live comfortably.

After interviewing several financial advisors, Ron and Charlotte met Trevor, a financial advisor they felt comfortable with. He assisted them with constructing a reasonably sized RRSP portfolio. Over the years, Trevor met with Ron and Charlotte to review their progress and assist them with budgeting based on their envisioned retirement needs. When Ron retired at sixty-five, he and Charlotte had over $700,000 set aside, which was enough to live comfortably and re-alize their retirement goals.

When asked about their progress, Ron and Charlotte admitted that without Trevor's professional advice and encouragement, they probably wouldn't have made the advances they did. If they had handled their finances themselves, Ron and Charlotte figured they would have likely given up and convinced themselves they were destined to work their entire lives. They agreed that even though they were relatively good money managers, they needed the outside advice and direction from someone like Trevor to help them realize their long-term retirement vision.

Net Worth Statement Worksheet

Assets

Cash on Hand	$_____
Cash in Checking	$_____
Cash in Bank or Credit Union	
Savings Account	$_____
Money Market Accounts	$_____
Market Value of Your Home	$_____
Estimated Value of	
Household Items	$_____
Market Value of Other Real Estate	
(i.e., investment or rental	
property, timeshare, vacation	
home)	$_____
Stocks	$_____
Bonds	$_____
Mutual Funds	$_____
Market Value of Vehicles	$_____
Cash Value Life Insurance	$_____
Current Value of RRSP	$_____
Current Value of TFSA	$_____
Estimated Value of Personal Items	$_____
Other Assets	$_____
Total Assets	$_____

Liabilities

Mortgage	$_____
Home Equity Loan or Line of Credit	$_____
Other Real Estate Loans	$_____
Auto Loan or Lease	$_____
Credit Card Balances	$_____
Student Loans	$_____
Delinquent Taxes	$_____
RRSP Loan	$_____
Personal Unsecured Loans	$_____
Life Insurance Loans	$_____
Other Liabilities	$_____
Total Liabilities	$_____

NET WORTH

(Assets minus Liabilities) $_____

Note from the Author

At the beginning of this book, I asked if you would simply live your retirement years with whatever happened or if you wanted something far better. From there, I invited you to take a journey to explore various aspects of retirement and construct a retirement plan tailored to meet your needs and match your vision. Much of this was and is inspired by successful retirees I meet as I travel throughout North America. In the course of many conversations, I repeatedly hear the importance of constructing and following a retirement vision and plan. Successful retirees underline the fact that having a well-thought-out vision acts as a compass during the transition into life after work. A retirement vision also acts as a touchstone for the decisions you'll need to make along the way.

I also have been gratified by all the retirees who share their experiences and advice with those who are now considering retirement. Remember, there are so many people out there who are more than willing to help. All you need to do is ask!

Your discoveries can also help others. I encourage you to drop me a note to share how your retirement plan is unfolding. Please let me know about your experiences, challenges, and successes as you progress down the retirement road. I will make your insights and words of wisdom available to others who follow in your footsteps.

I sincerely hope your journey will be thought-provoking and rewarding. I wish you the best in creating the best retirement you can.

Richard (Rick) Atkinson
ramgt@rogers.com
www.whencaniretire.info

References

Bebee, Gail. 2008. *No Hype: The Straight Goods on Investing Your Money*. Toronto: Ganneth.

Bolles, Richard N. 2013. *What Color Is Your Parachute? A Practical Manual for Job-Hunters and Career-Changers*. Berkeley: Ten Speed.

Bolles, Richard N. 2007. *What Color Is Your Parachute? for Retirement: Planning a Prosperous, Healthy, and Happy Future*. Berkeley: Ten Speed.

Cappon, Dick, and John R. Christensen. 2003. *Six Legs Jazz Club: A Journey to Uncovering Your Best Life*. Carp, ON: Creative Bound.

Chevreau, Jonathan. 2008. *Findependence Day: One Couple's Turbulent Journey to Financial Independence*. Toronto: Power Publishers.

Cooper, Sherry. 2008. *The New Retirement: How It Will Change Our Future*. Toronto: Penguin.

Diamond, Daryl. 2011. *Your Retirement Income Blueprint: A Six-Step Plan to Design and Build a Secure Retirement*. Mississauga: Wiley.

Gerber, Michael E. 2008. *Awakening the Entrepreneur Within: How Ordinary People Can Create Extraordinary Companies*. New York: HarperBusiness.

Gignac, Robert M. 2011. *Rich Is a State of Mind: Building Wealth and Happiness – A Blueprint*. Author's Choice.

Green, Lyndsay. 2010. *You Could Live a Long Time: Are*

You Ready? Toronto: Thomas Allen.

Holtzman, Elizabeth. 2002. *Emotional Aspects of Retirement*. Amherst: Amherst College.

Jaworski, Barbara. 2011. *Rebel Retirement: A KAA-Boomer's Guide to Creating and Living an Explosive Second Act*. Trafford.

Morton, Steven H. 2007. *Ten Common Mistakes Retirees Make*. iUniverse.

Oliver, Gene. 1999. *Life and the Art of Change*. LifeChange.

Petersen, Eric. 2015. *Preparing for the Back Nine of Life: A Boomer's Guide to Getting Ready for Retirement*. Charleston: Advantage.

Roadburg, Alan. 2002. *What Are You Doing After Work? A Retirement Lifestyle Planning Guide for Financial Advisors*. AGF Management.

Wigdor, Blossom T. 1985. *Planning Your Retirement: The Complete Canadian Self-Help Guide*. Toronto: Grosvenor.

About the Author

Richard (Rick) Atkinson, president of RA Retirement Advisors, is an expert in retirement planning. Known for his practical, interactive, and results-oriented workshops, he has helped people throughout North America plan for a successful and fulfilling retirement.

With over thirty-five years' experience as a human resource management specialist, Rick has worked as both an internal and external HR consultant in the manufacturing, oil and gas, mining, and health and social services sectors. He has also contracted his consulting services to municipal and provincial levels of government.

In addition to an M.B.A. from York University in Toronto and a B.Comm. (Hons) from the University of British Columbia in Vancouver, Rick holds the Ontario Society of Training and Development (now the Canadian Society of Training and Development) Advanced Level Certificate of Achievement.

Rick is a volunteer advisor for the Canadian Executive Service Organization (CESO) and for the past ten years has applied his mentoring skills to assist Inuit and non-Inuit as part of the Government of Nunavut's training and development initiative program.

Rick is happily married to Christine Edwards, and they are the parents of four daughters and the grandparents of eight grandchildren. Together, they are fulfilling their individual and shared retirement dreams in Toronto, Ontario, Canada.

CPSIA information can be obtained
at www.ICGtesting.com
Printed in the USA
LVOW04s0037290416
485834LV00012B/33/P